P9-CAE-752

THE
GLUTEN-FREE
INSTANT POT
COOKBOOK

Fast-to-Fix and Nourishing Recipes for
All Kinds of Electric Pressure Cookers

Jane Bonacci & Sara De Leeuw

HARVARD
COMMON
PRESS

Inspiring | Educating | Creating | Entertaining

Brimming with creative inspiration, how-to projects, and useful information to enrich your everyday life, Quarto Knows is a favorite destination for those pursuing their interests and passions. Visit our site and dig deeper with our books into your area of interest: Quarto Creates, Quarto Cooks, Quarto Homes, Quarto Lives, Quarto Drives, Quarto Explores, Quarto Gifts, or Quarto Kids.

© 2018 Quarto Publishing Group USA Inc.
Text © 2018 Jane Bonacci and Sara De Leeuw

First Published in 2018 by The Harvard Common Press, an imprint of The Quarto Group, 100 Cummings Center, Suite 265-D, Beverly, MA 01915, USA.
T (978) 282-9590 F (978) 283-2742 QuartoKnows.com

All rights reserved. No part of this book may be reproduced in any form without written permission of the copyright owners. All images in this book have been reproduced with the knowledge and prior consent of the artists concerned, and no responsibility is accepted by producer, publisher, or printer for any infringement of copyright or otherwise, arising from the contents of this publication. Every effort has been made to ensure that credits accurately comply with information supplied. We apologize for any inaccuracies that may have occurred and will resolve inaccurate or missing information in a subsequent reprinting of the book.

The Harvard Common Press titles are also available at discount for retail, wholesale, promotional, and bulk purchase. For details, contact the Special Sales Manager by email at specialsales@quarto.com or by mail at The Quarto Group, Attn: Special Sales Manager, 401 Second Avenue North, Suite 310, Minneapolis, MN 55401, USA.

22 21 20 19 18   1 2 3 4 5

ISBN: 978-1-55832-954-6

Digital edition published in 2018
eISBN: 978-1-55832-955-3

Library of Congress Cataloging-in-Publication Data available.

Cover Image: shutterstock.com
Illustration: shutterstock.com

Printed in China

SUSTAINABLE FORESTRY INITIATIVE
Certified Chain of Custody
Promoting Sustainable Forestry
www.sfiprogram.org
SFI-01268

SFI label applies to the text stock

This book has been written and produced for informational purposes only. Its content and suggestions are not a substitute for consultation with a physician. Medical and nutritional science changes rapidly, individuals have different sensitivity levels, and information contained in this book may not be current when read. Product recommendations were safe options as of the writing of this book. Manufacturers can change ingredients and processes without warning, so always read labels carefully. The reader assumes full responsibility for consulting a qualified health professional before starting a new diet or health program. Neither the publisher nor the authors are liable for any adverse reactions, consequences, loss, injury, or damage arising from information in this book, including loss or injury arising from typographical or mechanical errors.

To my loving husband James
for his unending love, support, and
sense of humor every day.
I wouldn't want to take this journey
with anyone else.
—Jane

To my husband, Steve; our children,
Matt, Amy, and Evan; and the Minis,
Harley and Joey.
Thank you for your love and
support of this crazy adventure.
I love you to the stars and back!
—Sara

CONTENTS

INTRODUCTION

Gluten-Free Cooking with an Electric Pressure Cooker

Hi there! Welcome to the wild and wonderful world of gluten-free pressure cooking. Pressure cooking is all the rage right now. However, if you're one of the millions of people who has a gluten allergy, gluten intolerance, or celiac disease, you may feel severely limited in your choices or as though you can't enjoy the pleasures of using a pressure cooker. We're here to show you that this is not the case. Pressure cookers allow you to cook fruits, vegetables, fish, meats, beans, rice, and alternative grains in no time. The possibilities are endless!

In this book, you will find fifty recipes that highlight the flavors and tastes of many classic and modern dishes, all without using wheat or other gluten-based ingredients. Every recipe in this book was developed with care and by keeping in mind our gluten-free loved ones. It's because of them that we know the challenges posed with eating gluten free, including how to create meals that are gluten free *and* delicious. So, we took some family favorites, did some research, made some changes to the ingredients, and let the pressure cooker work its magic. We were not disappointed!

Using a pressure cooker has provided new opportunities for gluten-free dishes that all of our friends and family members with food allergies (including gluten) can enjoy. After all, there shouldn't be any reason we can't have a great meal together. And since gluten ingredients have been added to so many commercially produced foods, you wind up having to make many items from scratch. Having ways to lessen the time needed to get a safe dinner on the table is a big help. Less hands-on time lets you relax and helps make cooking more fun. Having a book like this when we started cooking gluten free would have been a dream—so, we started writing.

We often hear: "I have a pressure cooker, but I've never taken it out of the box. I'm afraid of it!" We felt the same way! Pressure cookers can be intimidating. Some of us have memories from our childhood of the old-fashioned, clunky machines that sat on the stovetop. They made horrible hissing noises and had a round weight on top that rocked back and forth, spewing steam and spinning around. They were angry stovetop robots, and they were scary!

Today's modern, updated, electric pressure cookers are not the same pressure cookers used by our mothers and grandmothers. And thank goodness for that! There isn't anything scary about them.

Once you muster up the courage to try your electric pressure cooker, you'll quickly discover how much fun it is and how much it can benefit you in the kitchen. We absolutely love ours and rely on them heavily to get nutritious gluten-free dinners on the table and to prepare healthy lunches for the week. It will quickly become one of your favorite kitchen appliances.

As with any new appliance, there is a learning curve. If you burned toast the first time you used your toaster, did you give up? No, you kept going, adjusted some buttons, and tried again. It's the same thing with your electric pressure cooker. It gets easier with time and practice. Start simple, and soon you'll be making all kinds of incredible dishes.

This book will make you feel more comfortable, not only using your pressure cooker but also making tasty, gluten-free meals. We've given you guidance to help if you are new to a gluten-free diet or only cook occasionally, recommendations for gluten-free ingredients, and information you can use in all your gluten-free baking and cooking. Everyone, regardless of diet, can be a part of the pressure cooker revolution, and this book proves it! So, whether you are new to pressure cooking, new to gluten-free living, or are already an expert and simply want new recipes, we've got you covered. Come on, let's get cooking!

Why Use a Pressure Cooker?

There is a certain satisfaction in having dinner simmering away on the stove, filling the house with delicious smells. But what if there were a way to have that same dinner in a fraction of the time? With today's busy schedules and so many people on the go, using an electric pressure cooker can be a game-changer. We're excited to share with you everything it can do and how it's going to revolutionize the way you cook. Let's walk through some basic information about electric pressure cookers together and review some of the tools you'll want to be successful.

Pressure cookers have several benefits over more traditional cooking methods. Here are some of the top reasons to use a pressure cooker:

1. **Exceptional flavor and nutrition!** How food is prepared matters! Pressure cookers create a depth of flavor in your dishes like no other cooking method. They help retain the quality of the foods you cook by preparing them quickly and with very little water. Heat is distributed swiftly and allows flavor to penetrate into your food more deeply than with traditional cooking. The steam inside the pot allows meats to become moist and succulent and vegetables to retain their crispness, beautiful color, and, most importantly, their flavor. Vitamins and nutrients are better retained in foods cooked with a pressure cooker because they are cooked for a shorter amount of time. Less time means less opportunity for vitamins and minerals to be dissolved away, making food healthier and better for you.

2. **Food cooks quickly!** In a pressure cooker, the cooking time is greatly reduced. You can cook foods up to 70 percent faster than other conventional methods. This is a handy feature when you're trying to get dinner on the table in a short amount of time. You don't have to spend hours at the stove any longer. Because food is cooked so quickly, it still retains all the richness and natural flavors of foods cooked for hours in the oven. (See above!) You can make a pot of beans, a whole chicken, soups and stews, roasts, and rice so quickly and easily that the pressure cooker will be your new best friend in the kitchen.

3. **They are safe!** Electric pressure cookers are much safer than your grandmother's (or mother's) pressure cooker. Today's designs have numerous built-in safety features that ensure safe, successful meals without fear of the exploding pressure cookers of yesteryear. The pressure, heating, and sealing functions are all regulated, so you don't have to worry. Lids must be locked in place before pressure builds and won't open until pressure has been released. So there is absolutely nothing to worry about.

4. **They use less energy!** Electric pressure cookers take far less energy than cooking with multiple pots on your stovetop or hours in your oven. This can be a significant savings. With much less water used in cooking, it is also better for the environment. Because foods are cooked in far less time, less energy is needed to prepare meals. An added bonus? Electric pressure cookers won't heat up the kitchen when you use them.

5. **Cleanup is a breeze!** Cook in one pot and clean one pot. It doesn't get any easier. Cooking on your stovetop can leave splatters across your counters and walls, resulting in extra mess and more to clean. With an electric pressure cooker, everything is contained, and most of the time, you'll have only one pot and the lid to clean. And less mess means even less time spent in the kitchen. You'll have more time to spend with your kids or doing the things you love.

Finding the Perfect Pressure Cooker

Many brands offer "multifunction" pressure cookers, which can handle a multitude of different tasks. There is no need for several appliances taking up space on your counter. With today's multifunction electric pressure cookers, not only do you get a pressure cooker, but you also get a slow cooker, a rice cooker, a steamer, a warming pot, the ability to sauté and sear, and in some models you can even make your own yogurt. It's an all-in-one package.

With so many different electric pressure cookers on the market today, how do you know which is best for you? The decision about which brand to choose should be based largely on what you like to cook and how you will be using it. Some things to consider are the number of people in your household. If you have a large family, an 8-quart (7.2 L) model (or larger) might be best. If there are just two of you and you don't cook often, a 3- or 4-quart (2.7 or 3.6 L) version might be perfect. All the recipes in this book were written for a 6-quart (5.4 L) pressure cooker, and most often a 6-quart (5.4 L) will give you the most versatility, but choose the one that works best for you and your style of cooking.

Something else to take into consideration are the different functions each brand offers. Do you love yogurt? Make sure your model has a yogurt function. (Trust me, I speak from experience on this one. There are three pressure cookers in my house for a reason.) Does your family eat a lot of rice? Explore a brand that has a rice cooker function. Think all those buttons are too complicated for you? Buy one that is rated as exceptionally user-friendly.

How Do Pressure Cookers Work?

A pressure cooker is a sealed pot with a valve that controls the steam and pressure inside the pot. Pressure cookers work by heating liquids in a tightly sealed pot, which creates steam. As the liquid boils, the trapped steam raises the internal cooking temperature past the boiling point of water. The internal temperature of the pot can reach upwards of 250°F (120°C). The higher heat, and conversely higher pressure, forces liquid into the food and cooks it much faster than traditional methods. In fact, foods can be cooked up to 70 percent faster in a pressure cooker. Pressure-cooked foods become moist, juicy, and succulent. Tough fibers break down faster, so inexpensive cuts of meat become fork-tender in a very short amount of time. Dried beans don't need to be soaked for hours, and you can cook healthy, nutritious alternative grains in minutes.

The Parts of a Pressure Cooker

Though there are many different brands of electric pressure cookers on the market, they all have similar features. Here are some of the basics you'll find on every model:

Outer Housing Unit or Base: This is what holds the inner cooking pot. The display/control panel will be located on the outside. The control panel is where you will program your pressure cooker to cook. It will have all the function buttons and any preset programs. On the inside of the housing unit is the heating element. This is located at the base of the unit and looks like a ceramic disk. At the center of the heating element is a temperature sensor. The temperature sensor does just that—senses the temperature of your pressure cooker. It will automatically shut off if it senses the temperature inside the pot is too high.

Inner Cooking Pot: This is where the magic happens! Most brands have removable inner pots that are made of stainless steel, ceramic, or aluminum. These are almost all dishwasher safe, and that makes cleanup simple and easy! Always make sure your inner pot is in the housing unit before adding any liquid or ingredients to your pressure cooker. Some inner pots will have a "Max" fill line etched on the inside. This is another safety system for pressure cookers and ensures the food inside doesn't bubble up too far and clog the valves.

Lid: The lid of your pressure cooker is where you'll find the majority of safety features and all the cooking valves.

Pressure Release Valve: This is sometimes called a steam release handle, pressure limit valve, or pressure regulator knob. It is used to control the pressure inside your cooker. Generally, there are two positions for this valve. There is a "sealing" or "pressure" position. This is the position your pressure release valve should be in every time you begin cooking. It will seal in the steam and allow the pressure to build so you can cook dishes successfully. There is also a "venting" position, used after the cook time is complete to allow the built-up steam to escape. Occasionally these positions are marked on the exterior of the lid, but not always. When you release pressure from a pressure cooker, be aware that very hot steam is being expelled from your machine at a high rate. At no time should you put your face or hands near this steam. Burns from hot steam are quite painful, and we don't want you to get hurt.

Float Pin or Float Valve: This is one of the safety features on a modern electric pressure cooker. A tiny valve located on the lid of your appliance, it resembles a flat nail head. This valve gets pushed up by the steam inside your pot when the unit comes to pressure. The valve helps seal the cooker and prevents the lid from being opened while at pressure. When the float pin drops, it means the majority of pressure has escaped from the pot and you can carefully open the lid.

Sealing Ring: Also called a rubber gasket or silicone gasket, this removable ring is found under the lid of your pressure cooker. It's made of stiff food-grade silicone and forms a pressure-tight seal between the lid and the pressure cooker. This is removable, so you can take it out to clean it. Gaskets should be replaced every year or if they develop a thin spot.

The Display Buttons on the Control Panel

The display buttons on different brands, models, and sizes of electric pressure cookers all have their own functions. Each of those functions makes them unique and special. Many have programs built in for things like soup, grains, meats, eggs, or even cakes. When using these function buttons, the pressure cooker will cook for a specific amount of time at a specific pressure. The time and pressure settings cannot be changed. There is a simple convenience to being able to push a button and walk away. Know, too, that the pressure cooker can't tell what type of food is in the pot. If you use the "Poultry" button for cooking rice because you like how it turns out, no one will ever know.

Every pressure cooker will also have an option for setting the cooking time manually. It may be a button that actually says "Manual," or it might be labeled as something else. Get to know this button on your electric pressure cooker! Many recipes, including all the ones in this book, are written with instructions to "Press Manual and cook for XX minutes." This allows everyone the flexibility to use the same recipes, regardless of the brand or model of pressure cooker you own.

There will be a "Sauté" or "Browning" button that allows you to sear food before cooking it. This button works best for searing meats or sautéing vegetables. You can also use this function after cooking to thicken sauces and gravies. Some brands have a "Simmer" option, which you can use in any recipe that doesn't require the higher heat point of sautéing.

There will be a "Cancel/Keep Warm" button. This button will cancel any function currently in progress or simply turn off your pressure cooker. The "Keep Warm" part of the button allows you to keep food inside your cooker warm after the end of the cooking time. Some pressure cookers will let you decide whether you want to keep foods warm or have the cooker automatically shut off at the end of the cooking time. Read your manual to know whether your electric pressure cooker has this option.

Some pressure cookers feature multiple pressure settings, so you can choose to cook at high pressure or low pressure. Usually that setting is changed with + or - buttons located on the control panel.

Your electric pressure cooker will have a display timer that allows you to set the amount of time needed to cook. It will count down once the pot is at pressure and will show you how much cooking time is left before the food is done.

A locking lid is one of the most important safety features of modern electric pressure cookers. The lid cannot be removed while the pot is under pressure. If for some reason something were to go wrong with your pressure cooker, such as the valves were blocked or the electricity were to go out, your lid would remain locked until the pressure inside had decreased enough for the unit to be opened safely. Remember those horror stories about exploding pots and scraping food off the ceiling? This is likely because the lid was forced open on the pressure cooker without properly releasing the inside pressure. Locking lids mean today's electric pressure cookers don't have this problem.

Pressure Release Methods

There are three ways to release the pressure inside your electric pressure cooker: a quick release method, a natural release method, and a combination of the two.

Quick Pressure Release Method, or "QPR": This is when you release all the steam immediately after the cooking time ends. Do this by opening the steam handle to the "venting" or "steam" position and allow all the steam to escape before opening the lid. Depending on what you're cooking, this can take from 1 to 5 minutes.

Natural Pressure Release, or "NPR": This is when you allow your pressure cooker to release built-up pressure naturally. When the cooking time is complete, turn off your appliance and wait until the float pin drops and you can safely open the lid. This can take anywhere from 10 to 30 minutes.

You may be asked to do a controlled release, which is when you hold the release handle halfway between the sealing and venting positions, carefully releasing steam. With pasta, you have a lot of starch in the water that can make a mess of your kitchen. Controlling the pressure release allows you to limit the amount of splashing. Be sure to use a hot pad to protect your hands.

Combination of Natural Pressure Release and Quick Pressure Release: The recipe will call for a natural release for a specific amount of time and then a quick release of the remaining pressure before opening the lid. Example: "When the cook time is finished, allow a 10-minute natural release, then move the handle to the venting position and release any remaining steam. When the float pin drops, unlock the lid and open it carefully."

Regardless of which method your recipe requires, always make sure the float pin has dropped before opening the lid, and always open the lid away from you so you aren't accidentally burned by any residual steam.

Because models and brands vary widely, we strongly recommend you take the time to read the instruction manual that comes with your pressure cooker. It's important to know how your specific model works.

The Hot Water Test

Now that you are familiar with the basic parts of a pressure cooker, how it works, the safety features, and the pressure release methods, it's time to do an initial hot water test. This test is important and will enable you to see how your pressure cooker works. You'll get to see how quickly it comes to pressure, stays at pressure, and then releases pressure. Think of it as a troubleshooting test run. Basically, we're boiling water. We don't know about you, but we would much rather test something with a pot of water than be cooking a full meal and discover there may be a problem. Better to lose a few cups of water than a whole pot of expensive ingredients, right? Doing this test also gives you an opportunity to get comfortable with locking the lid in place, setting your pressure cooker, and using pressure release methods. Ready?

1. First, put the inner pot inside the housing unit. This is a good habit to get into so you don't accidentally pour water (or any other liquids/ingredients) into the housing unit by mistake.

2. Measure 3 cups (705 ml) water and pour it into the inner pot.

3. Inspect the lid to make sure the sealing ring is properly in place, then close and lock the lid.

4. Check to make sure the pressure release valve is closed. This is another good habit to have. Checking the valve every time you close the lid of your pressure cooker will save you from waiting forever for your cooker to come to pressure only to discover the release valve was open and now dinner will take even longer. Yes, we've done this. Many times. It's no fun.

5. Select Manual and set the timer on the control panel to cook for 5 minutes at high pressure.

6. Watch your unit carefully so you can see how it works. Take notes if you wish. It will take from 5 to 10 minutes for your unit to come to pressure. You may be able to hear the water inside begin to boil. You'll also see wisps of steam coming from the float valve. This is normal. The steam is what makes the float valve rise and seal. As you get to know your unit, you'll know when the valve seals because you'll hear a click or you'll notice a distinct lack of noise because the steam is no longer coming out. The timer will start once your unit is at pressure. This doesn't happen immediately after the float valve seals, but will begin within 1 to 2 minutes.

7. When the cook time is over, your unit will beep to let you know it's done. Carefully turn the pressure release valve to the open or venting position (some brands call it the Steam position) and allow the steam to escape. Remember, the steam is very hot and can burn you, so keep your face, hands, and arms away from it. It's also important to note which direction the steam is escaping. You may want to turn your pot so the steam doesn't hit the underside of a cabinet or any wall decorations you may have in your kitchen. If opening the pressure release valve makes you uncomfortable, you can use a pot holder or the handle of a long wooden spoon to gently move it to the open position.

8. Once the pressure and steam are released, you'll hear the float pin drop. On some models you can clearly see it drop back into the recessed position. This means the lid is unlocked and you can now open it safely.

9. Carefully open the lid, tilting it away from you so any residual steam and condensation that has collected under the lid doesn't drip on you or on the counter (or splash onto bare feet. Ouch!). There will always be condensation under the lid after cooking with a pressure cooker. When you open the lid, position it so the water drips back into the pot, instead of going elsewhere.

10. The inner pot will be hot. Use silicone mitts, pot holders, or a kitchen towel to remove it from the housing unit. Measure the amount of water left in the pot. You should see very little difference from the 3 cups (705 ml) water you added in the beginning. You may have lost 1 tablespoon (15 ml) or so, but nothing much above that. In a pressure cooker there is very little liquid lost to evaporation.

11. At this point, if you have chosen a brand that has a Keep Warm setting, you'll see the timer may have begun to count up. Press Cancel or unplug your machine. Different brands/models will allow you to turn off the Keep Warm setting so that when the cook time is over, the pressure cooker simply turns itself off. Either way, be sure to unplug your appliance when you're finished.

That's it! You have successfully done your water test and are ready to create delicious meals for your whole family.

Basic Equipment

Trivet: A trivet or steam rack often comes standard with many electric pressure cookers. This rack keeps food, bowls, and pans elevated off the bottom of the inner cooking pot. This is an essential tool in your pressure-cooking arsenal. We also suggest purchasing a long-leg trivet that will fit in your pressure cooker. This is useful for several of our pot-in-pot recipes, as it allows more food to be underneath and still be able to keep another pot balanced safely above.

Steamer Basket: Generally speaking, when we say "steamer basket," we are referring to a collapsible basket made of stainless steel with overlapping side leaves that can be expanded to fit inside most 6- or 8-quart (5.4 or 7.2 L) pressure cookers. It has a colander-type basket and has feet, so it can be used to hold vegetables or proteins over boiling water to steam them. The center post, which occasionally has a ring on the end of it, can be used to help lift the basket from the inner pot. The center post is also removable, which makes it perfect for steaming larger vegetables like whole artichokes or spaghetti squash. You can find steamer baskets made of silicone or smaller baskets that double as strainers and come with lift handles that also fit easily inside most 6-quart (5.4 L) or larger pressure cookers.

Instant-Read Thermometer: (We recommend Thermapen from ThermoWorks.) An instant-read thermometer helps you check to ensure larger cuts of meats have been cooked to a safe internal temperature. It is also beneficial in ensuring your yogurt (if your pressure cooker has that function) has reached the proper temperature.

Portable Timer: Another product sold by ThermoWorks is a portable timer called a TimeStick. It is very convenient to set the timer, hang it around your neck, and be able to do chores in other parts of the house knowing you won't miss the alarm!

A 7 x 3-Inch (18 x 7.6 cm) Springform Pan or Push Pan: This is great to use for cheesecakes and lasagna. The sides of a springform pan expand and then buckle closed. It has a detachable bottom, which makes removing cheesecakes simple and easy. A push pan (we like Fat Daddio's) also has a removable bottom, but the sides of the pan are solid, so removing things like lasagna is nearly effortless.

A 7 x 3-Inch (18 x 7.6 cm) Round Cake Pan: We use this pan a lot. If you can afford only one additional pan, make it this one. It's useful for cakes, spinach dip, frittatas, meatloaf, and pot-in-pot rice. If necessary, this pan can also be used for lasagna, but you will have difficulty removing your food.

A 6-Cup (1440 g) Bundt Pan: This half-size Bundt pan (we love Nordic Ware) fits perfectly inside most 6-quart (5.4 L) electric pressure cookers. Use it for cakes or bread pudding!

Small 4-Ounce (112 g) Mason Jars: These are sometimes called quilted jelly jars and are perfect for making individual-size cheesecakes or desserts.

Flat Wooden Spatula or Turner: This utensil helps release any browned bits off the bottom of the pot when you sauté your food and easily breaks up clumps of cooking ground meat.

A 1½-Quart (1.4 L) Round Ceramic Casserole Dish without Handles: This is a great dish to have. It can double as a rice dish for pot-in-pot meals. It will fit a batch of Spinach Artichoke Dip (page 34) perfectly and fits seamlessly inside a 6-quart (5.4 L) pressure cooker.

Additional Silicone Rings: You will need to replace your sealing ring (sealing gasket) at least once a year. Thankfully they are not expensive. Some people have different colored gaskets that they switch out regularly for use when making sweet dishes versus savory dishes. The gaskets do tend to pick up odors, and who wants a cheesecake that smells like spaghetti and meatballs?

Aluminum Foil Sling: One of the best tools you will use with your pressure cooker is an aluminum sling. It will help you lift pans in and out of the pressure cooker with ease. The great thing about an aluminum sling? It is not expensive and you can use it over and over again. I keep mine in the same drawer as my plastic storage bags and parchment paper. First, tear off a sheet of aluminum foil about 24 inches (61 cm) long and lay it out on the kitchen table. Fold it lengthwise evenly into thirds, much like you were folding a piece of paper to put in an envelope. Run your hands over the edges to flatten it. Center the pan you want to lift in the middle of your newly created sling. Fold the edges up around the pan and bring the ends together. Twist the ends together to create a handle. Now you can safely place pans inside your pressure cooker without spilling the contents and, more importantly, you can lift hot pans out of the pressure cooker without burning your fingers. Some people like to create two slings for extra support on each side of the baking dish.

Silicone Pinch Mitts: Small, heat-resistant oven mitts designed to protect your hands and fingers from the hot inner cooking pot, these mitts allow you to grip the edges of the pot without getting burned. Most come with a textured grip surface to reduce the risk of slipping.

Retriever Tongs: These are different than traditional kitchen tongs. Retriever tongs are great for taking a very hot dish out of a container. They are designed to clip and lift the inner pot or steamer basket from your pressure cooker. They are also useful for taking hot plates from the oven or microwave without having to touch them.

Jar Lifter Tongs: This is a tool used often in canning. It is essential for lifting hot jars out of a water bath canner. It is also very useful for getting individual jars of cheesecake out of your pressure cooker.

Special Equipment and Accessories

Immersion Blender: This is a powerful stick blender. It is lightweight with sharp blades, and you can use it to blend foods right in your pressure cooker. You can mash potatoes, blend sauces, process hummus, and more. It usually comes with a whisk attachment and some kind of bowl or beaker, which also makes blending sauce or pesto easy and convenient.

An 8 x 4-Inch (20.3 x 10.2 cm) Loaf Pan: Instant Pot has a springform silicone loaf pan that fits beautifully inside their 6-quart (5.4 L) electric pressure cookers. It's handy to bake more traditional meatloaf or quick breads.

Kitchen Scale: We recommend the OXO Good Grips Food Scale with an 11-pound (5 kg) capacity. This is especially important for your gluten-free baking needs. This scale will allow you to measure in both U.S. and metric increments. It has a zero function, which allows you to tare the scale with a bowl or other container before measuring so you'll have accurately measured ingredients every time.

Tips for Using Your Pressure Cooker Successfully

Always read the instruction manual that comes with your pressure cooker. It may seem boring or unnecessary, but the manuals are written for a reason. It's critical to your success to know your pressure cooker's strengths and limitations.

Be aware of recipes and timing. This is imperative to keep in mind when planning your meals. Cooking in a pressure cooker is fast, but it does take time to put together. Always read through the entire recipe, sometimes twice. There is nothing worse than starting a recipe only to realize you are missing an essential ingredient. Consider the time it takes to prep your ingredients, then the time it takes for your pressure cooker to come to pressure. The same way an oven must preheat, pressure cookers need time to heat up and begin to build steam and pressure to cook your food. Also factor the total recipe cooking time and any specific pressure release time into your planning. A "3-minute" recipe might actually take 20 to 25 minutes depending on the temperature of your ingredients and how much liquid is in your pressure cooker.

Altitude can make a difference! Because pressure cookers are built on the principle of boiling water to create steam, it's important to know that water boils at lower temperatures at higher elevations. For pressure cookers, shorter cooking times at a higher elevation is generally not a problem, but for longer cooking times or specific foods like grains or beans, you may need to make adjustments. A good, basic rule to follow is to add 5 percent more cooking time for each 1,000 feet (305 m) after 3,000 feet (915 m) above sea level. So if you live at 4,000 feet (1220 m), you would add 10 percent; at 5,000 feet (1524 m), add 15 percent; and so on. If you aren't sure, always use a food thermometer to help determine the temperature of your food. If you need to make adjustments from there, then you can do so safely. *Note:* All the recipes in this book were tested at or near sea level.

Always ensure you have enough liquid in the inner pot to bring it to pressure. The minimum amount of liquid will vary depending on the brand of electric pressure cooker. Generally speaking, this is at least 1 cup (235 ml) of liquid, but check with your owner's manual and always use tested recipes. Some recipes may call for less liquid because the food you are cooking releases a lot of water during the cooking process. An example is our Sweet Spiced Applesauce (page 126). It only requires ¼ cup (60 ml) of liquid.

Do not overfill your pressure cooker. Pressure cookers require space for steam to build pressure and cook properly. A basic guideline is no more than two-thirds full for most recipes and half full for foods such as beans and grains, as they tend to expand and foam during cooking. Overfilling a pot can also create hazards and clog your vent pipes and valves. If your vents and valves get dirty, you'll need to clean them so your cooker can properly come to pressure.

If you hear popping noises, don't worry. This is common. Popping noises happen when the heating unit goes from one temperature to another and can happen occasionally if the bottom of your inner pot is wet. Be sure to dry it completely before starting to cook.

Some steam coming from the release valve is normal. Small wisps of steam will happen as the unit is coming to pressure before the float valve seals. However, if large plumes of steam continue for more than 2 minutes, check the valve to make sure it is set to sealing, not venting. If that doesn't fix the problem, you may have food debris on the float pin blocking the valve from sealing. Simply clean it according to your manufacturer's instructions and try again.

Brown meats or vegetables first, then deglaze the pot for more flavor. Most recipes will ask you to add oil or butter to the inner cooking pot and then brown or sauté an ingredient. Add the food in small batches and evenly brown the food on all sides. Remove the food to a serving plate or bowl, then use water, broth, or whatever liquid is specified in the recipe to loosen up and remove those delicious, cooked-on food particles left on the bottom of the pan. This is a great flavor enhancer for your dishes.

Follow instructions for thickening sauces. Many recipes designed for pressure cookers call for thickening the sauces and gravies after cooking. This is because pressure cookers use liquid to create steam and that liquid needs to be thin. Adding flour is a common way to thicken that flavorful cooking liquid in your pressure cooker, but being gluten free means that is not an option. Instead, we use alternative thickeners. A cornstarch slurry (a mixture of cornstarch and water), arrowroot powder, or tapioca starch are good options for use in a pressure cooker. If your recipe calls for white beans, you can also blend ¼ cup (60 g) beans with ¼ cup (60 ml) of the cooking liquid into a bean slurry and use it to thicken soups and stews. Simmering the sauces until they're reduced is another option.

Our Recommended Flour Blend and Other Gluten-Free Flour Blends

When you are baking or cooking certain recipes, you will need to use a gluten-free all-purpose flour. If you will be baking a lot, making your own blend in bulk will save you money. If you are only using it occasionally, feel free to use a store-bought brand. Some of our favorites are Bob's Red Mill 1-to-1 Baking Flour, Pamela's All-Purpose Gluten-Free Flour, King Arthur Gluten-Free All-Purpose Flour, Cup4Cup Gluten-Free Flour Blend, and Authentic Foods' Gluten-Free Classical Blend.

In addition to gluten-free flours, a blend needs starches to give structure and lift to your baked goods. Starches are nearly always included, but it is not a given that the blend you buy includes gums or psyllium husk powder. Gums help hold your baked goods together and keep them from crumbling. If your commercial blend includes xanthan gum (or guar gum), reduce the amount called for in recipes by half. If you are sensitive to gums, you can use psyllium husk powder for the same purpose. Just use double the amount. So if the recipe calls for 1 teaspoon xanthan gum, replace that with 2 teaspoons psyllium husk powder.

To make it easier for you, we have included our favorite all-purpose blend to use in any baking and cooking recipes, both from this book and from other sources.

ALL-PURPOSE GLUTEN-FREE FLOUR BLEND

When you are baking or making recipes that call for flour, having a gluten-free blend already made and available is helpful. Use 120 grams for every 1 cup of flour called for in any recipe. This blend does not contain any dairy, nuts, or gums, making it very versatile. You can use it in everything calling for flour.

INGREDIENTS

280 g (9.9 ounces, or 2 cups plus
   2 tablespoons) sweet rice flour
   (not white rice flour)

280 g (9.9 ounces, or 2 cups plus
   5 teaspoons) brown or white rice flour

120 g (4.2 ounces, or 1 cup plus
   4¾ teaspoons) tapioca flour/starch

120 g (4.2 ounces, or ¾ cup) potato
   starch (not potato flour)

METHOD

1. Whisk the ingredients together and store in a large food-safe plastic bin. Secure the lid on the container and shake vigorously to distribute all the ingredients evenly.

2. Gluten-free flours tend to settle and sometimes separate while sitting, so always shake the container well before measuring for each baking project.

Yield: 1.8 pounds, or about 6 cups (800 g)

BEGUILING BREAKFASTS

We always hear, "Breakfast is the most important meal of the day," and it's true. It puts fuel in our tank and wakes up our brain, giving us the energy we need to be effective and successful every day.

Steel-cut oats take a really long time to cook on the stove, but when you use your electric pressure cooker, they can easily be made for hungry family members on school days. Just be sure to use a certified gluten-free brand. I love that they hold texture and stay chewy, the perfect way to wake up on cold days.

Frittatas are an Italian omelet-like egg preparation made in a pan inside the pressure cooker. With the steam, they bake into a soufflé-like texture. With their tender and delicate perfection, they make a lovely centerpiece for any brunch or breakfast. Grits are a classic in the American South, and our version is packed with savory flavors of sausage, cheese, and jalapeño. This is another dish guaranteed to fill up the hungriest folks at your table.

If you are looking for a healthy meal on busy mornings, try our Sweet Potato and Egg Caribbean Breakfast Burritos (page 28). It's filled with delicious flavors and ingredients and wrapped in a gluten-free tortilla, so you can eat this quickly and still have a healthy breakfast. Starting your day with a good meal will make every day brighter!

CHEESY POBLANO FRITTATA

Gluten Free • Vegetarian • Soy Free • Nut Free

Frittatas are a quick and easy breakfast, brunch, or midweek dinner option. The cumin and peppers add flavor and a little heat, which takes this in a Southwestern direction. You can pass hot sauce at the table if you have guests who like spicier foods. Serving a tossed green salad alongside makes a healthy, light meal.

INGREDIENTS

1 tablespoon (15 ml) olive or vegetable oil

¼ cup (40 g) finely chopped onion

2 poblano peppers, seeded and finely chopped

1 red bell pepper, cored, seeded, and finely chopped

1 tablespoon (1 g) finely minced fresh cilantro leaves, plus more for garnish

½ teaspoon ground cumin

6 large eggs

1 cup (235 ml) half-and-half

½ teaspoon kosher or fine sea salt

¼ teaspoon freshly ground black pepper

1 cup (120 g) shredded Colby or cheddar cheese, divided

For the cooking pot

1½ cups (355 ml) water

If you are using a springform or push pan, wrap the outside of the pan with foil to ensure the liquid remains inside the pan. The foil on top also helps keep most of the steam from collecting in the bottom of the pan.

METHOD

1. Spray a 7 x 3-inch (18 x 7.6 cm) round baking pan with nonstick vegetable cooking spray (do *not* use the kind with flour in it). Tear off a piece of foil large enough to cover the pan and spray one side of it with the cooking spray.

2. Press Sauté on your electric pressure cooker. Add the oil to the inner pot. When shimmering and hot, add the onion and peppers. Cook, stirring often to coat with the oil, until softened, about 5 minutes. Stir in the cilantro and cumin. Press Cancel. Transfer the vegetables to a bowl.

3. Wipe out the inner pot, return it to the pressure cooker, place a trivet in the bottom, and pour in the water.

4. In a bowl, whisk together the eggs, half-and-half, salt, and pepper. Stir in the cooked onions and peppers and ¾ cup (90 g) of the cheese. Pour into the prepared baking pan. Sprinkle the remaining ¼ cup (30 g) cheese over the top. Cover the top with the foil, sprayed side down, crimping it around the edges of the pan. Use a sling (see page 15) to lower it into the inner pot.

5. Close and lock the lid, making sure the steam release handle is in the sealing position. Cook on high pressure for 20 minutes. When it is finished, release the pressure naturally for 10 minutes, then turn the steam release handle to venting, releasing any remaining steam. Unlock the lid and open it carefully.

6. Use the sling to lift the pan out of the pot. Set on a wire cooling rack and carefully remove the foil. Use a paper towel to pat any excess liquid off the top of the frittata. If you want, you can put the pan under the broiler to add color to the top.

7. Cut into wedges, use a spatula to move the pieces to serving plates, and sprinkle the top with additional chopped cilantro if desired. Serve hot.

Yield: 4 servings

CREAMY STEEL-CUT OATMEAL WITH APPLE RAISIN COMPOTE

Gluten Free • Vegetarian • Soy Free • Nut Free • Egg Free

This breakfast treat is a cross between old-fashioned oatmeal and an apple pie with a hit of cinnamon to wake up your taste buds. Warm and comforting, it is the perfect way to start your day.

When you cook with regular oats, you run the risk of cross-contamination due to how they are grown and processed. But if you buy certified gluten-free oats, you can eat them with confidence. Bob's Red Mill offers gluten-free oats that can be found at grocery stores and are also available for purchase online at www.bobsredmill.com.

INGREDIENTS

For the compote

1 tart apple, such as Granny Smith

1 sweet apple, such as Golden Delicious

3 tablespoons (30 g) golden raisins (optional)

½ cup (120 ml) orange juice or apple juice

2 teaspoons (10 ml) freshly squeezed lemon juice

2 tablespoons (30 g) brown sugar

2 tablespoons (30 ml) maple syrup

½ teaspoon ground cinnamon

½ teaspoon gluten-free vanilla extract

½ teaspoon fresh lemon zest

For the oatmeal

Butter, for greasing

3 cups (705 ml) water

2 cups (470 ml) milk or dairy-free milk of your choice

2 cups (160 g) steel-cut oats (do not use regular rolled or instant oats)

Pinch of kosher or fine sea salt

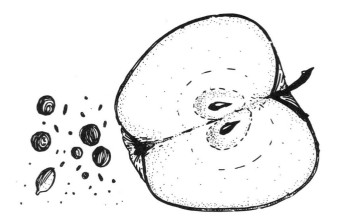

METHOD

Compote

1. Peel and core the apples and cut into small chunks. Place in a saucepan. Add the raisins, orange juice, lemon juice, brown sugar, maple syrup, cinnamon, vanilla, and lemon zest. Stir to combine. Cook over medium heat, stirring occasionally, until the apples are fork-tender and the liquid is syrupy. Transfer the compote to a bowl and set aside.

Oatmeal

1. Lightly butter the bottom and lower sides of the inner pot to help avoid sticking. Add the water, milk, oats, and salt, but do *not* stir. Close and lock the lid, making sure the steam release handle is in the sealing position. Cook on high pressure for 9 minutes. When it is finished, release the pressure naturally, which will take about 15 minutes. Turn the steam release handle to venting, releasing any remaining steam. Unlock the lid and open it carefully.

2. Scoop the oatmeal into bowls and top with a tablespoon or two of the fruit compote. Serve immediately.

Yield: 4 to 6 servings

SAUSAGE AND JALAPEÑO CHEESE GRITS

Gluten Free • Soy Free • Nut Free • Egg Free

On a trip to Georgia, we were treated to our host's famous grits. Each morning, we would head to the kitchen and watch as he proudly made his specialty. This recipe is packed with flavor from sausage, jalapeño peppers, and cheese. Healthy and filling, these grits gave us energy for our days of sightseeing in the beautiful wooded back roads of Georgia.

INGREDIENTS

3 tablespoons (45 ml) olive or vegetable oil, divided

½ pound raw (227 g) mild Homemade Sausage (page 27)

¼ cup (40 g) finely chopped onion

½ jalapeño pepper, finely minced, or more to taste

1 cup (140 g) stone-ground grits (*not* instant grits)

3 cups (705 ml) cool water

1½ cups (355 ml) half-and-half or heavy cream

2 teaspoons (12 g) kosher or fine sea salt

1 cup (120 g) shredded cheddar cheese, divided

Many folks will resort to using quick grits to save time on busy days. With today's electric pressure cookers, you can enjoy the superior flavor of long-cooked stone-ground or coarse-ground grits prepared in a fraction of the time.

METHOD

1. Press Sauté and heat 1 tablespoon (15 ml) of the oil in the inner pot of your electric pressure cooker. When it is hot, add the sausage and cook, stirring often, until completely browned. Break up any clumps that form, keeping the pieces small and easy to eat. Add the onion and jalapeño and stir to combine. Cook for about 3 minutes to soften the vegetables. Transfer to a bowl and set aside.

2. Add the remaining 2 tablespoons (30 ml) oil and the grits to the inner pot and cook, stirring often, for 1 minute, until the oil has been absorbed and the grits are lightly toasted. Stir in the water, half-and-half, and salt. Press Cancel.

3. Close and lock the lid, making sure the steam release handle is in the sealing position. Cook on high pressure for 10 minutes. When it is finished, release the pressure naturally for 10 minutes, then turn the steam release handle to venting, releasing any remaining steam. Unlock the lid and open it carefully.

4. Whisk the grits until smooth. If they are too thick and heavy, add a tablespoon (15 ml) milk or more as needed to get a creamy texture. Stir the sausage mixture into the grits. Add half the cheese and stir until it is melted. Scoop into serving bowls and top with remaining cheese. Serve immediately.

Yield: 4 servings

Homemade Sausage

Sausage often contains gluten fillers, but by making it yourself, you can control the purity of the ingredients, the percentage of fat, and the seasonings.

2 teaspoons (12 g) minced parsley

1 teaspoon kosher or fine sea salt

1 teaspoon rubbed sage

1 teaspoon dried thyme

1 teaspoon gluten-free chili powder, optional

1 teaspoon freshly ground black pepper

1 teaspoon dried basil leaves

1 teaspoon dried oregano

⅓ cup (55 g) grated onion

2½ pounds (1.1 kg) ground pork or a combination of ground pork and ground turkey

1. Combine the herbs and spices in a small bowl.

2. Place the onion and meat in a large bowl. Add the seasoning blend and mix together with your hands until evenly distributed.

3. Divide the mixture into two or three sections and roll each one into a log. Wrap the logs individually in plastic wrap and refrigerate overnight or freeze for longer storage. When ready to use, slice into patties or use in bulk.

Yield: 2½ pounds (1.1 kg)

SWEET POTATO AND EGG CARIBBEAN BREAKFAST BURRITOS

Gluten Free • Dairy-Free Option • Soy Free • Nut Free

Easy and quick breakfast options are always popular, and these Caribbean-influenced burritos are no exception. Filled with chunks of sweet potatoes, black beans, scrambled eggs, and salsa, they are satisfying and a great way to kick off busy days.

INGREDIENTS

For the potatoes

1 cup (235 ml) water or vegetable stock (page 137)

½ pound (227 g) sweet potatoes, peeled and cut into small cubes

Kosher or fine sea salt and freshly ground black pepper

For the filling

2 tablespoons (30 ml) olive or vegetable oil, divided

½ onion, finely chopped

½ red bell pepper, seeded and finely chopped

1 teaspoon chipotle powder

1 cup (240 g) canned gluten-free black beans, rinsed and drained

6 large eggs

For assembly

4 large gluten-free tortillas, such as Mission gluten-free brand, warmed (see Note)

½ cup (120 g) gluten-free salsa, such as tomatillo, salsa verde, salsa roja, or pico de gallo

1 cup (120 g) shredded Monterey Jack, pepper Jack, or Colby cheese

Freshly squeezed lime juice

Fresh cilantro leaves, chopped

METHOD

Potatoes

1. Pour the water into the bottom of the inner pot of your electric pressure cooker. Place a steamer basket in the pot and pile the potatoes in the basket. Close and lock the lid, making sure the steam release handle is in the sealing position. Cook on high pressure for 2 minutes. Naturally release the pressure for 2 minutes, then quick release the remaining pressure by turning the steam release handle to venting. Press Cancel. Unlock the lid and open it carefully. Lift the potatoes out of the pot, season with salt and pepper, set aside, and keep warm. The potatoes can be cooked a day ahead and rewarmed before cooking the eggs and assembling the burritos.

Filling

1. While the potatoes are cooking, in a 10-inch (25 cm) skillet, heat 1 tablespoon (15 ml) of the oil and cook the onion and pepper for 5 minutes to soften slightly. Add the chipotle powder and beans to the skillet, heating through. Use a slotted spoon to transfer the vegetables to a bowl and cover to keep warm.

2. Add the remaining 1 tablespoon (15 ml) oil to the skillet. Beat the eggs in a bowl until blended, then pour into the skillet and cook, stirring constantly, until scrambled. Remove the pan from the heat. Using a spatula, chop the eggs into small pieces. Stir the beans and vegetables into the eggs and keep warm.

Assembly

1. Lightly warm the tortillas (see Note) and layer one-fourth of the potatoes and one-fourth of the eggs on each one. Top with 2 tablespoons (30 g) of the salsa and about ¼ cup (30 g) of the shredded cheese. Sprinkle with some lime juice and a little cilantro, carefully roll up, and serve while warm. If they are delicate and tending to tear, eat them with a fork.

NOTE: Warm the tortillas in a dry skillet or the microwave to make them pliable. If they are cold, they will crack when you try to fill and roll them. Be aware, gluten-free tortillas can be quite delicate. It is safest to eat these over a plate to catch anything that may fall out.

Yield: 4 servings

To make this a low-carb meal, turn this into a burrito bowl by leaving off the tortilla. Scoop the filling into bowls and eat with a fork.

APPEALING APPETIZERS

Every great party starts with great food! You don't have to give up on nibbles and tidbits because of dietary restrictions. With your pressure cooker it's easy to create tantalizing dips and more substantial individual bite-size treats. Skip the store-bought versions of these classic appetizers in favor of your own gluten-free alternatives. We promise not to tell if you have more than one serving!

For a crowd, we suggest the Cherry Chipotle Chicken Wings (page 36) or a big batch of Hummus (page 32) with plenty of vegetables for dipping. Having a more intimate party? Go for the Steamed Artichokes with Spicy Garlic Aioli (page 40) or pass a plate of Delightfully Delicious Deviled Eggs (page 38).

Whether you're celebrating with friends, hanging out to watch the game, or hosting a family gathering, these fast and friendly, crowd-pleasing appetizers allow you to celebrate without having to worry about watching the stove or what may be hiding in the ingredients list.

HUMMUS

Gluten Free • Dairy Free • Vegetarian

An added bonus of cooking beans in a pressure cooker means you don't have to soak them. With a little bit of extra time, they cook up perfectly, no soaking required. Make this deliciously easy hummus while the chickpeas are still warm and you'll have a smooth, light dip to serve with vegetables or gluten-free crackers.

INGREDIENTS

1 cup (240 g) dried chickpeas

3 cups (705 ml) water

1 teaspoon salt

3 tablespoons (45 ml) olive oil, plus more for serving

¼ cup (60 g) tahini

3 tablespoons (45 ml) lemon juice

4 cloves garlic, chopped roughly

1 teaspoon ground cumin

Salt and pepper to taste

Smoked paprika, for serving

Chopped fresh parsley, for serving

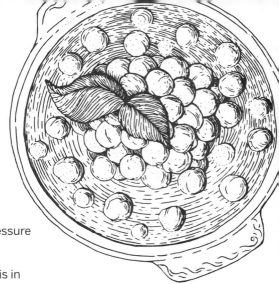

METHOD

1. Add the dried chickpeas to the inner pot of your electric pressure cooker. Add the water and salt.

2. Close and lock the lid, making sure the steam release knob is in the sealing position. Cook on high pressure for 60 minutes. When the cook time is finished, allow a complete natural release. When the float pin drops, unlock the lid and open it carefully.

3. Ladle 1 cup (235 ml) of the cooking liquid out of the pot and set it aside. Using mitts or a dish towel, carefully lift out the inner pot and drain the chickpeas into a colander.

4. Transfer the warm, drained chickpeas to a food processor or blender. Add the olive oil, tahini, lemon juice, garlic, cumin, and salt. Process at medium speed, slowly adding in the reserved cooking liquid. Continue until the mixture is smooth and creamy. If needed, stop and scrape down the sides of the bowl and process again to achieve the desired texture. You might not use all of the cooking liquid.

5. Taste the hummus. Adjust the seasoning with salt and pepper, if needed.

6. Serve with a drizzle of olive oil and a sprinkle of smoked paprika and parsley. Store in an airtight container for up to 5 or 6 days.

Yield: 2 cups (480 g)

SPINACH ARTICHOKE DIP

Gluten Free • Soy Free • Nut Free • Vegetarian

A must-have game-day appetizer, this dip will easily feed a crowd. This time-honored, highly addictive dip is a blend of cheesy goodness that uses ingredients you probably have in your pantry. We love that you put everything together in your mixer and then cook it in the pressure cooker. This dip goes together as quickly as it will disappear and makes a great quick snack for a stay-at-home movie night, too!

INGREDIENTS

1 (10-ounce, or 280 g) package frozen spinach, thawed, chopped, and well drained

1 (14-ounce, or 392 g) can artichoke hearts, drained and coarsely chopped

4 cloves garlic, minced

½ cup (80 g) finely chopped onion

1 (8-ounce, or 227 g) block cream cheese, softened to room temperature and cut into cubes

1 cup (100 g) grated Parmesan cheese

1 cup (120 g) shredded mozzarella cheese

½ cup (120 g) sour cream or plain Greek yogurt

½ teaspoon salt

¾ teaspoon freshly ground black pepper

⅛ teaspoon cayenne pepper

2 cups (470 ml) water

Gluten-free crackers, for serving

METHOD

1. In a large bowl, or the bowl of your stand mixer, combine the spinach, artichokes, garlic, onion, cream cheese, Parmesan, mozzarella, sour cream, and seasonings. Mix well until thoroughly incorporated.

2. Spoon the mixture into a lightly greased 1½-quart (1.4 L) baking dish or a 7 x 3-inch (18 x 7.6 cm) cake pan that will fit in your pressure cooker. Cover the baking dish tightly with foil.

3. Place a trivet at the bottom of the inner pot of your pressure cooker and add the water.

4. Using a foil sling (see page 15), carefully lower the casserole dish into the pressure cooker. Fold the foil strips down so that they do not interfere with closing the lid.

5. Close and lock the lid, making sure the steam release knob is in the sealing position. Cook on high pressure for 10 minutes. When the cook time is finished, use a quick release by opening the release knob and venting all the steam. When the float pin drops, unlock the lid and open it carefully.

6. Remove the foil-covered dish with the sling and check the dip to make sure the cheese is completely melted. Stir to combine. If you like a crispy top, slide the casserole dish under the broiler for 2 minutes until the cheese is a golden brown color. Watch carefully so it doesn't burn.

7. Serve warm with gluten-free crackers.

Yield: 10 servings

CHERRY CHIPOTLE CHICKEN WINGS

Gluten Free • Dairy Free • Nut Free • Soy Free • Paleo • Vegetarian

This will quickly become your favorite party appetizer! The chicken wings get a little crispy when you sauté them, but then are steamed to tender perfection in your pressure cooker. The sauce has a sweet and spicy kick your whole family will enjoy. I love that there are just a few ingredients in this recipe, so you can make it any time unexpected guests pop in! If you can't find Not Ketchup, simply substitute your favorite gluten-free BBQ sauce (such as Stubb's brand).

INGREDIENTS

¼ cup (56 g) butter

1 cup (240 g) Not Ketchup Cherry Chipotle Sauce (or your favorite gluten-free BBQ/hot wing sauce)

1 tablespoon (15 ml) vegetable oil

3 to 4 pounds (1362 to 1816 g) chicken wings

Salt and pepper to taste

1 cup (235 ml) chicken stock (page 136)

Gluten-free ranch dressing, for serving

Carrot and celery sticks, for serving

You can buy Not Ketchup sauces online at Amazon. They have a variety of different flavors, including a Spiced Fig and a Tangerine Hatch Chile that would also work well with this recipe. Check out their regular Fruitchup, Smoky Date, and Blueberry White Pepper, too! They are all gluten free, dairy free, and soy free!

METHOD

1. In a small saucepan, melt the butter over low heat, then add the chipotle sauce. Cook over low heat, whisking continuously to combine. Simmer gently for 6 to 8 minutes, or until the sauce begins to thicken. Set aside.

2. Press Sauté on your electric pressure cooker. When the inner pot is hot, add the oil. Place the chicken wings in the pot and season with salt and pepper. Brown them for 5 minutes on each side. Remove to a serving plate.

3. Pour the chicken stock into the inner pot. Use a wooden spoon to gently scrape up any browned bits from the bottom of the pan.

4. Place a trivet in the bottom of the cooking pot over the stock. Place the browned wings on the trivet, being careful not to let the wings touch the broth.

5. Close and lock the lid, making sure the steam release knob is in the sealing position. Cook on high pressure for 5 minutes. When the cook time is finished, allow a 5-minute natural release, then do a quick release to vent any remaining steam. When the float pin drops, unlock the lid and open it carefully.

6. Line a baking sheet with aluminum foil. Remove the chicken wings from the pressure cooker and place on the lined baking sheet. If you have a rack that fits in the baking sheet, even better! The air circulating around the wings as they sit on the rack will make your wings extra crispy. If you don't have a rack, just put the wings on the foil-lined baking sheet. They will still get crispy.

7. Generously brush the wings with the warm sauce and broil for 7 minutes on each side. If they are not crispy enough, broil for 2 to 3 minutes more on each side.

8. Remove from the oven and, if desired, toss the wings quickly in the remaining sauce. Serve with gluten-free ranch dressing alongside some carrot and celery sticks.

Yield: 6 servings

DELIGHTFULLY DELICIOUS DEVILED EGGS

Gluten Free • Dairy Free • Soy Free • Nut Free • Vegetarian • Paleo

One of the most wonderful things about an electric pressure cooker is the ability to cook hard-boiled eggs. Steaming the eggs under pressure creates the best, easy-to-peel eggs you've ever had. If you have ever lost half the egg white because the peel stuck, this method will make you love making them again. This classic variation of traditional deviled eggs adds hot sauce for a spicy kick!

INGREDIENTS

For the hard-boiled eggs

1 cup (235 ml) cold water

12 large eggs, straight from the refrigerator

Large bowl of water with ice

For the deviled eggs

12 hard-boiled eggs

2/3 cup (160 g) mayonnaise

1 tablespoon (6 g) dry mustard powder

2 teaspoons (10 ml) hot sauce

Salt and pepper to taste

Smoked paprika, for garnish

Scallions, sliced on the diagonal, green parts only, for garnish

METHOD

Hard-boiled eggs

1. Pour the cold water in the inner cooking pot. Place a steam rack or trivet in the inner pot of your pressure cooker. Place the eggs on the trivet.

2. Close and lock the lid, making sure the steam release knob is in the sealing position. Cook on high pressure for 6 minutes (depending on how soft or firm you like the yolk). Naturally release the pressure for 6 minutes, then unlock the lid and open it carefully. Turn off the machine.

3. Remove the eggs and immediately plunge them into the bowl of ice water to stop the cooking. Let them sit for 6 to 10 minutes. If serving immediately, peel the eggs under running water. Store unpeeled eggs in the refrigerator up to 1 week.

Deviled eggs

1. Peel the hard-boiled eggs and slice in half. Remove the yolks and set aside.

2. In the bowl of a food processor, pulse hard egg yolks until they resemble yellow sand. Add the mayonnaise, mustard, and hot sauce. Blend until the mixture is smooth and creamy. If you don't have a food processor, combine the ingredients in a medium bowl and use a hand mixer to get the desired consistency. Add salt and pepper to taste.

3. Fill the hollows of the egg whites with the yolk mix. Sprinkle with smoked paprika and scallions to garnish.

Yield: about 24 servings

STEAMED ARTICHOKES WITH SPICY GARLIC AIOLI

Gluten Free • Nut Free • Soy Free • Vegetarian

Artichokes are full of fiber and high in antioxidants, plus they taste great! There is a tiny restaurant on the beach in Moss Landing, California, that serves fresh steamed artichokes from a nearby farm to local beachgoers. Eating them, dipped in a spicy garlic aioli, while enjoying the sun and sand is a decadent treat. The aioli has just enough garlic to give it a pleasant zing, but feel free to add more if you are a garlic lover! This recipe can be used as an appetizer to feed several people or can be made into a special meal for two.

INGREDIENTS

For the artichokes

3 medium artichokes

1 whole lemon, cut into quarters

1 cup (235 ml) water

¼ cup (60 ml) lemon juice

3 cloves garlic, smashed

For the spicy garlic aioli

3 tablespoons (45 g) plain Greek yogurt

2 tablespoons (30 g) mayonnaise

4 cloves garlic, minced

½ teaspoon cayenne pepper

¼ teaspoon garlic powder

½ teaspoon coarsely ground black pepper

Pinch of salt

If the spicy garlic dip isn't for you, make a simple dip with melted butter, a bit of dill, and some grated Parmesan cheese.

METHOD

Artichokes

1. Use a serrated knife to cut the top third off each artichoke. Cut the stems off at the base. Rinse the artichokes well. Rub one of the lemon quarters all over the cut tops of the artichoke to prevent them from browning.

2. Add the lemon quarters, water, lemon juice, and garlic to the pot. Place a steam rack or trivet in the inner pot of your pressure cooker. Place the artichokes on the trivet.

3. Close and lock the lid, making sure the steam release knob is in the sealing position. Cook on high pressure for 10 minutes. When the cook time is finished, use a quick release method. Move the release knob to the venting position and vent all the steam. When all the steam has been expelled and the float pin drops, unlock the lid and open it carefully.

4. Pull off an artichoke leaf to test for doneness; it should come off without any resistance. Carefully lift the artichokes from the inner pot of your pressure cooker with a pair of tongs. Set aside to cool while you make the aioli.

Aioli

1. In a medium bowl, combine all the ingredients for the aioli and whisk until smooth.

2. Serve the artichokes on a plate with the aioli.

Yield: 6 servings

SPECTACULAR SOUPS AND STEWS

Soups and stews are some of the best and easiest things to make in your pressure cooker. The pressure tenderizes even the hardest ingredients, like butternut squash, in a fraction of the time and beans are cooked so quickly you almost don't have time to make the garnishes.

Because there is no evaporation during cooking, there will be less liquid called for in these recipes than you are accustomed to seeing. This helps concentrate the flavors and avoids having the soups and stews become watered down. One way to intensify the flavors is to use bouillon, soup base, or demi-glace. These are highly concentrated granules and pastes you can add by the spoonful. Most bases contain gluten, so be careful to get a gluten-free variety. Herb-Ox brand has a line of gluten-free bouillons that are quite good.

It is very important to never fill the pot above the maximum fill line on the inner pot. You need room at the top of the pot. Also, the more liquid you have in the pot, the longer it will take to come to pressure and to release—it always takes longer for a large pot of water to come to a boil.

If you want to thicken your soups and stews a bit, you can always turn on Sauté, bring the mixture to a boil, and reduce the liquid with the lid off. For more thickening power, try using a starch. Because you can't stir while the lid is locked on, avoid using a gluten-free flour added during cooking, like dredging meats in flour and browning before cooking. The best solution is to thicken the liquid after cooking by adding a cornstarch slurry, which is cornstarch dissolved in cool water. If you cannot have corn products, use half as much potato starch (*not* potato flour) as called for in the recipe.

BEEF "BARLEY" SOUP WITH SORGHUM

Gluten Free • Dairy Free • Soy Free • Nut Free

One of the most-missed soups for those who can no longer have gluten ingredients is beef barley soup. It was challenging finding anything that could approximate the flavor and texture of the barley, but sorghum is extremely versatile and makes a good substitute. It can be ground into a flour that is delicious in breads and other baked goods. It can be turned into a syrup that brings back memories of simpler times. And you can use it whole, which, when cooked, becomes a tantalizingly chewy grain that is reminiscent of barley.

INGREDIENTS

2 tablespoons (30 ml) olive or vegetable oil

1½ pounds (680 g) beef chuck roast, fat trimmed and meat cut into 1-inch (2.5 cm) cubes

1 large onion, chopped

2 cloves garlic, minced

2 carrots, trimmed and chopped

2 stalks celery, trimmed and chopped

1 tablespoon (15 g) tomato paste

1 teaspoon minced fresh rosemary leaves

1 teaspoon fresh thyme leaves

6½ cups (1528 ml) beef stock (page 134) or gluten-free store-bought broth (see Note)

1 cup (200 g) whole-grain sorghum, rinsed and drained

2 bay leaves

Kosher or fine sea salt and ground black pepper, to taste

Whole-grain sorghum can be challenging to find. If it isn't readily available in your local grocery store, you can order it online from Bob's Red Mill (www.bobsredmill.com).

METHOD

1. Press Sauté and pour the oil into the inner pot of your electric pressure cooker. Brown the beef on all sides, working in batches so you can leave room between the pieces as they cook. Transfer the browned beef to a plate; set aside.

2. Add the onion and garlic to the oil in the pot. Cook, stirring often, until the onion has begun to soften, about 3 minutes. Stir in the carrots, celery, tomato paste, rosemary, and thyme. Cook for another 3 minutes, stirring regularly. Pour in the stock and scrape the bottom of the pan to release any browned bits. Add the sorghum and bay leaves. Return the beef to the pot. Press Cancel.

3. Close and lock the lid, making sure the steam release handle is in the sealing position. Cook on high pressure for 40 minutes. When it is finished, release the pressure naturally for 10 minutes, then turn the steam release handle to venting, releasing remaining steam. Unlock the lid and carefully open.

4. Taste the broth and adjust the seasoning with salt and pepper as desired. Remove and discard the bay leaves. Ladle into bowls and serve.

NOTE: Using homemade stock lets you control the amount of salt in your dishes. If you use canned beef stock, it will likely be saltier than homemade. If you taste the soup and it is too salty, you can add more water to dilute it.

Yield: About 4 servings

BLACK BEAN SOUP WITH CILANTRO-LIME CREAM

Gluten Free • Dairy-Free Option • Vegetarian • Vegan Option • Soy Free • Nut Free • Egg Free

There are meals we experience in our lives that leave a lasting impression. The first time we had black bean soup was on a chilly afternoon at the renowned Chez Panisse in Berkeley, California. The soup had deeply layered flavors, and we loved the contrasting creaminess of the topping swirled into the soup. This black bean soup will fill you up and warm you on stormy days and with luck will help you create your own wonderful memories.

INGREDIENTS

For the soup

2 cups (480 g) dried black beans

2 tablespoons (30 ml) olive oil

1 large onion, finely chopped

1 large red bell pepper, cored, seeded, and finely chopped

2 stalks celery, trimmed and finely chopped

1 clove garlic, minced

1 tablespoon (3 g) dried oregano

1 tablespoon (6 g) ground cumin

1½ teaspoons kosher salt

½ teaspoon freshly ground black pepper

½ to 1 teaspoon chipotle powder, to taste

4 cups (940 ml) vegetable stock (page 137) or water, divided

Juice of ½ to 1 fresh lime

For the cilantro-lime cream (omit for dairy free and vegan)

¾ cup (180 g) sour cream

Juice of ½ to 1 fresh lime

¼ cup (4 g) fresh cilantro leaves, rinsed well and patted dry

½ to 1 teaspoon chipotle powder, to taste

Kosher or fine sea salt and ground white pepper, to taste

For optional garnishes

Chopped fresh cilantro leaves

Chopped scallion

Chopped ripe tomatoes

Fresh lime wedges

METHOD

Soup

1. Sort the beans, discarding any pebbles or debris, rinse them well, and drain. Place in a large bowl and cover with fresh water. Loosely cover and set aside overnight. Drain before adding to the soup. (See Note.)

2. Press the Sauté button on your electric pressure cooker. Add the oil to the inner pot and when hot, add the onion, bell pepper, and celery. Cook, stirring often, until the vegetables have softened, about 4 minutes. Add the garlic, oregano, cumin, salt, pepper, and chipotle powder. Stir to evenly coat all the vegetables with the seasonings. Add 1 cup (235 ml) of the stock, scraping the bottom of the pot to release any browned bits. Pour in the remaining 3 cups (705 ml) stock and the soaked and drained black beans; stir well. Press Cancel.

3. Close and lock the lid, making sure the steam release handle is in the sealing position. Cook on high pressure for 12 minutes.

When you are working with dried beans, be very careful to check for small stones or bits of rock. It is common to find some in nearly every bag. Spread the beans out on a baking sheet with sides, which will contain them. Working in sections, sort through all of the beans, discarding any debris you find. Rinse the beans well and drain before continuing with the recipe.

Cilantro-Lime Cream

1. Combine the sour cream, lime juice (start with juice of ½ lime), cilantro, and chipotle powder in a food processor. Run the motor until the herbs are completely pureed and smooth. Taste and add salt and pepper. Add more lime juice or cilantro if you want a bolder, brighter flavor, but remember that flavors intensify over time. Transfer to a bowl and set aside.

Finish the Soup

1. When the soup is finished, release the pressure naturally for 10 minutes, then turn the steam release handle to venting, releasing any remaining steam. Unlock the lid and open it carefully.

2. Use an immersion blender to puree the soup or transfer to a blender and puree in batches. You can leave some of the beans whole for a chunkier texture or puree until completely smooth. Stir in the fresh lime juice. Taste and adjust the seasonings. Ladle into serving bowls, add a dollop of the cream (if using), top with your desired garnishes, and serve.

NOTE: If you forgot to soak the beans overnight, don't worry, you can still make the soup. Place the sorted beans in a sauce pot and add enough water to cover by 3 inches (7.6 cm). Bring to a boil and cook for 1 minute. Turn off the heat, cover, and let the beans rest for 1 hour. Drain and cook as directed above.

Yield: About 6 servings

SPICY BUTTERNUT SQUASH SOUP

Gluten Free • Dairy Free • Vegetarian • Vegan • Soy Free • Nut Free • Egg Free

This butternut squash soup is silky smooth, savory with a touch of sweetness, and has a surprising pop of spice. It is just the right meal on a rainy or snowy day. Imagine enjoying a bowl while sitting in front of a roaring fire. One bite and you and your family will be craving this soup all winter long!

INGREDIENTS

1 large butternut squash

3 tablespoons (45 ml) olive or vegetable oil, divided

2 large shallots, minced

3 stalks celery, trimmed and finely chopped

2 carrots, trimmed and finely chopped

2 teaspoons fresh thyme leaves

2 cloves garlic, minced

3 cups (705 ml) vegetable stock (page 137) or gluten-free store-bought broth, divided

2 tablespoons (30 ml) maple syrup or agave syrup, or to taste

1 teaspoon kosher or fine sea salt

½ teaspoon freshly ground black pepper

¼ teaspoon hot sauce, or to taste (Sriracha brand is gluten free)

Chopped chives, for garnish

To make this even easier and save you time, you can buy the squash already cleaned and cubed at many grocery stores. This takes care of the bulk of the chopping and lets you relax and let the pressure cooker do all the work!

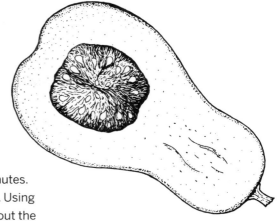

METHOD

1. Place the squash in the microwave and heat for 1 to 2 minutes. This softens the rind and makes it easier and safer to cut. Using a large, sharp knife, cut the squash into quarters, scrape out the seeds and strings, and peel the chunks. Cut into cubes.

2. Press Sauté and add the oil to the inner pot. When it is hot, add the shallots, celery, carrots, and thyme and cook 4 minutes, stirring often, or until softened. Add the garlic and cook for 30 seconds. Add 1 cup (235 ml) of the stock to the pot, scraping the bottom to release any browned bits. Add the remaining 2 cups (470 ml) stock, maple syrup, salt, pepper, hot sauce, and butternut squash. Press Cancel.

3. Close and lock the lid, making sure the steam release handle is in the sealing position. Cook on high pressure for 9 minutes. When it is finished, release the pressure naturally for 10 minutes, then release the remaining pressure by turning the steam release handle to venting. When the pressure valve drops, unlock the lid and open it carefully. Check to make sure the squash is fork-tender. If it needs more time, replace the lid, return to pressure, and cook for another 2 or 3 minutes.

4. Use an immersion blender to puree the soup right in the inner pot, or transfer half of the soup at a time to a blender and puree in batches. Taste the soup and adjust the seasonings as needed. If the soup is too thick, add a little more stock or water. Ladle into serving bowls, sprinkle with the chives, and serve hot.

Yield: 4 to 6 servings

DREAMY CREAMY TOMATO SOUP

Gluten Free • Vegetarian • Soy Free • Nut Free • Egg Free

One bite of this soup and you will be transported back to childhood, sunny days, scraped knees, and braces. Packed with bold tomato flavor enhanced with herbs and vegetables, this soup definitely doesn't come out of a can! Don't be surprised when your family and friends beg you to make this soup over and over again.

INGREDIENTS

2 tablespoons (28 g) butter or (30 ml) olive oil, divided

1 medium onion, finely chopped

3 carrots, finely chopped

3 stalks celery, finely chopped

½ red bell pepper, seeded and finely chopped

1 clove garlic, minced

2 cups (470 ml) chicken stock (page 136)

About 50 ounces (1500 g) chopped or crushed tomatoes, such as Pomi brand

2 teaspoons (1 g) dried oregano

2 teaspoons (1 g) dried basil

½ teaspoon dried crushed rosemary

1 bay leaf

1 teaspoon granulated sugar

2 teaspoons (12 g) kosher or fine sea salt

1 teaspoon freshly ground black pepper

½ cup (120 ml) heavy cream or half-and-half

2 tablespoons (4 g) finely minced fresh basil leaves, plus whole leaves for garnish

When a recipe highlights an ingredient like this recipe does tomatoes, it pays to use the best you can afford. Pomi brand tomatoes are imported from Northern Italy and are consistently high quality for the best-tasting recipes. They come in boxes and can be found at many major grocery stores across the nation.

METHOD

1. Press Sauté and heat the inner pot of your electric pressure cooker. Melt 1 tablespoon (14 g) of the butter. Add the onion, carrots, celery, and bell pepper and cook for 3 minutes, stirring, to soften. Stir in the garlic and cook for 30 seconds. Add the stock, tomatoes, herbs, sugar, salt, and pepper. Stir to combine. Press Cancel.

2. Close and lock the lid, making sure the steam release handle is in the sealing position. Cook on high pressure for 5 minutes. When it is finished, release the pressure naturally for 10 minutes, then turn the steam release handle to venting, releasing any remaining steam. Unlock the lid and open it carefully. Press Cancel.

3. Remove and discard the bay leaf. Stir in the remaining 1 tablespoon (14 g) butter and stir until it is melted. Use an immersion blender to puree the soup in the pot. You can also use a blender, but puree in batches—hot liquids expand!

4. Stir in the cream and chopped basil. Taste and adjust the seasonings if needed. Ladle into bowls, garnish with basil leaves, and serve.

Yield: About 4 servings

PUMPKIN
BLACK BEAN CHILI

Gluten Free • Dairy Free • Soy Free • Vegan • Vegetarian

Don't let the pumpkin keep you from making this delicious chili. Not only does it add nutrients, but it also makes for a thick, hearty dinner on cold winter nights. The peppers in the chili are easily customizable for your family, too. For a hotter chili, add more jalapeños or chipotle peppers. For a less spicy, kid-friendly version, bell peppers are a perfect substitute. Serve with avocado slices, fresh lime wedges, and some chopped cilantro scattered over the top of each bowl.

INGREDIENTS

1 (28-ounce, or 784 g) can fire-roasted diced tomatoes, including juice

1 large poblano pepper, seeded and finely chopped

2 jalapeño peppers, seeded and minced

1 chipotle pepper from canned gluten-free chipotle in adobo, chopped

1 medium yellow onion, minced

4 cloves garlic, minced

1½ cups (210 g) chopped walnuts, toasted

2 cups (400 g) red lentils

1 tablespoon (15 ml) sauce from chipotles in adobo, or more depending on your heat preference (La Costeña brand is gluten free)

2 teaspoons (12 g) salt

3 tablespoons (24 g) gluten-free chili powder (Penzey's and McCormick clearly label their products)

2 tablespoons (14 g) smoked paprika (Penzey's brand is gluten free)

7 cups (1645 ml) vegetable stock (page 137), divided

1 (14-ounce, or 392 g) can pumpkin puree (*not* pie filling)

2 (15-ounce, or 438 g) cans black beans, well rinsed and drained

For optional garnishes

Avocado slices

Lime wedges

Chopped fresh cilantro

Savory Gluten-Free Corn Bread (page 110)

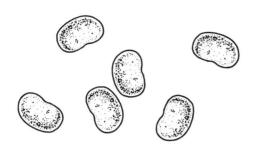

Red lentils have been hulled and split, showing their lovely golden-orange color. They are easier to cook and make for a very smooth consistency.

METHOD

1. Place the tomatoes, peppers, onion, garlic, walnuts, lentils, and seasonings in the inner pot of your electric pressure cooker. Stir in 6 cups (1410 ml) of the vegetable stock.

2. Close and lock the lid, making sure the steam release knob is in the sealing position. Cook on high pressure for 30 minutes.

3. When the cooking time is complete, do a quick release by opening the release knob and venting all the steam. When the float pin drops, unlock the lid and open it carefully.

4. Stir in the pumpkin puree, black beans and ½ cup (120 ml) of remaining stock. Lock the lid back in place and allow the beans to warm through, about 5 minutes. If the chili is too thick, add the remaining ½ cup (120 ml) stock and stir well.

5. Serve with avocado, lime wedges, cilantro, and corn bread as desired.

Yield: 6 servings

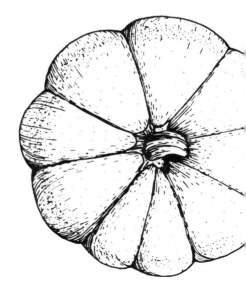

RIB-STICKIN' CHILI

Gluten Free • Dairy-Free Option • Soy Free • Nut Free • Egg Free

This is one of the easiest recipes to make in your electric pressure cooker and a real crowd-pleaser. Sauté the meats and veggies, put everything in the pot, and cook it. There is no stirring or babysitting required, and you get bold, long-cooked flavor in under an hour!

INGREDIENTS

2 tablespoons (30 ml) olive or vegetable oil

1 pound (454 g) lean ground beef

1 pound (454 g) bulk gluten-free ground sausage or Homemade Sausage (page 27)

1 large onion, diced

3 carrots, trimmed and diced

2 poblano peppers, seeded and diced

1 bell pepper, cored, seeded, and diced

2 jalapeño peppers, seeded and minced (see Note)

1 (28-ounce, or 794 g) can diced tomatoes with their juice

½ cup (120 ml) gluten-free beef stock (page 134) or water

1 tablespoon (15 ml) Worcestershire sauce (Lea & Perrins brand is gluten free)

¼ cup (32 g) chili powder (Penzey's brand is gluten free)

1 tablespoon (3 g) dried oregano

2 teaspoons (4 g) smoked paprika

1 teaspoon chipotle powder (optional)

1 teaspoon garlic powder

1 teaspoon ground cumin

2 teaspoons (12 g) kosher or fine sea salt

1 teaspoon freshly ground black pepper

2 tablespoons (16 g) masa harina or corn flour (Bob's Red Mill brand is gluten free)

¼ cup (60 ml) cool water

Optional toppings and accompaniments

Gluten-free corn tortillas, such as Mission brand

Sliced jalapeño peppers

Shredded cheddar cheese or dairy-free cheese

Minced red onion

Lime wedges

Sour cream or dairy-free sour cream

Chopped fresh parsley or cilantro

Traditional Texas chili has no beans in it, and this version doesn't either. For those who love beans in their chili, you can add gluten-free canned black beans, kidney beans, or pinto beans that have been rinsed and drained. Two (15-ounce, 428 g) cans will be filling and delicious. Stir them in at the end when you add the masa harina so they have time to warm up.

METHOD

1. Press Sauté on your electric pressure cooker and heat for 30 seconds. Add the oil and the meats and cook, stirring to break up clumps, until no pink is visible. Stir in the onion, carrots, poblanos, bell pepper, and jalapeños. Cook, stirring, for 3 more minutes. Stir in the tomatoes, stock, Worcestershire, and seasonings, scraping the bottom of the pot to release any browned bits. Press Cancel.

2. Close and lock the lid, making sure the steam release handle is in the sealing position. Cook on high pressure for 30 minutes. When it is finished, release the pressure naturally for 12 minutes, then turn the handle to venting and release the remaining pressure. Unlock the lid and open it carefully. Press Cancel.

3. Press Sauté. Dissolve the masa harina in the water, whisk it into the chili, and cook, stirring often, for 3 to 5 minutes, or until the chili thickens to the consistency you like. Taste and adjust the seasonings. Press Cancel.

4. Ladle into bowls and serve with gluten-free corn tortillas and your favorite toppings.

NOTE: If you like spicy foods, you can add chopped serrano or habanero peppers or more chipotle powder to the chili. Remember that seasonings get stronger as they rest, so start with a lighter hand and increase the amounts slowly.

Yield: 4 to 6 servings

GREAT GRAINS AND RICE

Whole grains have been feeding civilizations for centuries across the globe. They are a plentiful and inexpensive way to feed families. In addition to healthy fiber and nutrients, they add wonderful texture to your meals. One of the most challenging aspects of giving up gluten is losing favorite grains like barley, bulgur, and farro. Trying new-to-you grains can enhance your diet and help fill in the gaps left by gluten-full grains. Sorghum, millet, quinoa, and rice will have you reimagining what you think about when you hear the term *grains*.

Sorghum has a hearty, chewy texture and mild, nutty flavor that makes it perfect for use in pilafs, salads, and anywhere whole grains are on the ingredients list. It originated in Africa and is still a staple and source of nutrition in India and Africa. It can even be popped like popcorn! Millet was first cultivated nearly 10,000 years ago in China. It has a neutral, slightly sweet flavor and is a delicious alternative for salads, porridge, and stir-fries. When ground into a flour, it is beautiful in baked breads.

Quinoa, which is actually a seed, has gotten a lot of press lately and is becoming a go-to alternative grain. It has been a staple for thousands of years in the high reaches of the Andes Mountains in South America, and a sacred crop of the ancient Incans. High in fiber and protein, quinoa is a lovely option for vegetable salads and in soups. Rice comes in many different forms, giving you a multitude of textures, from soft and creamy to firm.

You are welcome to use these recipes as a guideline for how to make them in a pressure cooker and reinterpret your family's favorites.

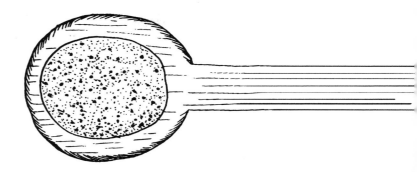

BROWN RICE PILAF

Gluten Free • Dairy Free • Vegetarian • Vegan • Soy Free • Nut Free • Egg Free

A pilaf is both a technique and a dish. You coat the rice with oil and sauté it briefly before adding liquids and finishing the cooking. Cooking rice with vegetables and aromatics helps the taste penetrate deeply into each grain, creating intense flavor in every bite. This pilaf makes a beautiful side dish to any main course.

INGREDIENTS

2 tablespoons (30 ml) olive or vegetable oil

1 medium onion, finely chopped

1 red bell pepper, cored, seeded, and finely chopped

2 stalks celery, trimmed and finely chopped

2 carrots, peeled, trimmed, and finely chopped

1 cup (180 g) raw brown rice (see Note)

1 teaspoon minced garlic

¼ cup (60 ml) dry white wine or water

1¼ cups (295 ml) vegetable stock (page 137) or water

½ teaspoon dried thyme

½ teaspoon kosher or fine sea salt

¼ teaspoon freshly ground black pepper

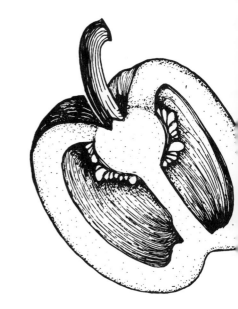

METHOD

1. Press Sauté on your electric pressure cooker. Heat the oil in the inner pot until shimmering. Add the onion, pepper, celery, and carrots. Cook, stirring often, until the onion is softened, about 3 minutes. Pour in the rice, stirring to coat all the grains with the oil. Continue cooking for about 5 minutes, or until the rice begins to smell nutty. Stir in the garlic and cook for 30 seconds. Add the wine, stirring to scrape up any browned bits from the bottom of the pot. Pour in the stock. Stir in the thyme, salt, and pepper. Press Cancel.

2. Close and lock the lid, making sure the steam release handle is in the sealing position. Cook on high pressure for 22 minutes. When it is finished, release the pressure naturally for 12 minutes, then turn the steam release handle to venting, releasing any remaining steam. Unlock the lid and open it carefully.

3. If there is any excess liquid present, press Sauté and cook the rice to evaporate it. Use a fork to fluff the rice. Taste and adjust the seasonings if needed. If it needs more cooking, replace the lid and let it rest for 5 minutes.

NOTE: If you want to make this dish with white rice, it will take just 3 minutes. Decrease the vegetable broth to 1 cup (235 ml). The rest of the recipe remains the same.

Yield: 4 servings

SAVORY CREAMY POLENTA

Gluten Free • Dairy-Free Option • Vegetarian/Vegan Option • Soy Free • Nut Free

Polenta is pure comfort food that can be served plain, sweetened, or as a base for savory meals. With brown sugar or maple syrup, it is the perfect way to start your day, and a great replacement for Cream of Wheat cereal. Topped with an Italian ragu, it is a luscious and filling meal. And it is a great side dish with grilled meats. This is another grain that takes a long time on the stove but quickly softens perfectly in your electric pressure cooker.

INGREDIENTS

1 cup (164 g) polenta or medium-grind cornmeal

4 cups (940 ml) water or vegetable stock (page 137)

1 teaspoon kosher or fine sea salt

¼ cup (60 ml) heavy cream or half-and-half (optional)

½ cup (50 g) grated Parmesan cheese (optional)

Polenta and other cornmeal preparations will stick to the cooking pot if it is not immediately rinsed. Never wait too long to fill the pot with soapy water or your cleanup will be much more challenging.

METHOD

1. Place the polenta, water, and salt in the inner pot of your electric pressure cooker. Stir well. Close and lock the lid, and make sure the steam release handle is in the sealing position before cooking on high for 5 minutes. When it is finished, allow the pressure to release naturally for 12 minutes. Then turn the steam release handle to venting, releasing any remaining steam. Unlock the lid and open it carefully.

2. Stir well with a whisk until the mixture becomes creamy and smooth, being sure to break up lumps. If desired, stir in the cream for additional richness. Scoop into bowls, sprinkle with the cheese, if using, and serve.

NOTE: For a sweet version, use water and no cheese. Top bowls of cooked polenta with brown sugar or maple syrup just before serving.

Yield: About 4 servings

MILLET AND CHICKEN GREEK SALAD

Gluten Free • Dairy-Free Option • Soy Free • Nut Free • Egg Free

Millet is a gluten-free grain that is similar to couscous or quinoa, with a touch of nuttiness in every bite. When combined with these Greek-inspired ingredients, it makes a delightful salad that wakes up your taste buds and is perfect for summer picnics or potlucks all year long.

INGREDIENTS

For the salad

2 tablespoons (30 ml) vegetable or olive oil

½ cup (80 g) very finely chopped onion

1 red bell pepper, cored, seeded, and very finely chopped

1 cup (175 g) millet, rinsed well and drained

½ teaspoon kosher or fine sea salt

½ teaspoon freshly ground black pepper

1 teaspoon dried oregano

1 cup (235 ml) water

¾ cup (180 ml) chicken stock (page 136) or water

1½ cups (60 g) baby spinach leaves, rinsed very well, shaken dry

1 small cucumber, peeled and finely chopped

⅓ cup (35 g) chopped olives, preferably Kalamata

⅓ cup (50 g) quartered cherry tomatoes

½ small red onion, very thinly sliced

1½ cups (210 g) cooked chicken (see page 84), cut into small cubes or shredded, at room temperature

For the dressing

⅓ cup (80 ml) extra virgin olive oil

2 tablespoons (30 ml) freshly squeezed lemon juice

1 to 2 tablespoons (15 to 30 ml) red wine vinegar, to taste

½ teaspoon kosher or fine sea salt

¼ teaspoon freshly ground black pepper

For topping

2 tablespoons (6 g) finely chopped fresh parsley

¼ cup (38 g) crumbled feta cheese (optional)

METHOD

Salad

1. Press Sauté and heat the vegetable oil in the inner pot of your electric pressure cooker. When it is shimmering, add the chopped onion and bell pepper and cook, stirring, for 4 minutes, or until the onion is slightly softened. Add the millet. Sprinkle with the salt, pepper, and oregano, then pour in the water and stock, stirring to be sure nothing is stuck to the bottom of the pot. Press Cancel.

2. Close and lock the lid, making sure the steam release handle is in the sealing position. Cook on high pressure for 9 minutes. When it is finished, release the pressure naturally for 8 minutes, then turn the steam release handle to venting, releasing any remaining steam. Unlock the lid and open it carefully.

3. Remove the lid, rake the grains with a fork, and transfer to a large bowl. Add the spinach to the bowl, stir it into the millet, and let the steam wilt the greens. Set aside to cool to room temperature, tossing occasionally with forks to help keep the millet from clumping. When cooled, stir in the cucumber, olives, tomatoes, red onion, and chicken.

Dressing

1. In a small bowl, whisk together the olive oil, lemon juice, vinegar, salt, and pepper. Pour half the dressing over the salad, tossing to coat all the ingredients. Taste and adjust the seasonings; add the remaining dressing if desired and toss again. Sprinkle the parsley and feta over the top and serve.

Yield: About 4 servings

PERFECT RICE
EVERY TIME

Gluten Free • Dairy Free • Vegetarian • Vegan • Soy Free • Nut Free • Egg Free

---

All rice is not created equal. Each type—short grain, medium grain, or long grain—will cook slightly differently, so use these directions as a guide. This technique is designed for when you buy rice in bulk where there are no directions to guide you. If you have a package with cooking directions on it, cut the cooking time in half and you will be very close to the right timing. Always make a note of changes so you can make adjustments the next time.

INGREDIENTS

For white rice

1 cup (180 g) long-grain white rice

1¼ cups (295 ml) water or vegetable stock (page 137)

½ teaspoon kosher or fine sea salt, or to taste

For brown rice

1 cup (190 g) brown rice

1½ cups (355 ml) water or vegetable stock (page 137)

½ teaspoon kosher or fine sea salt, or to taste

Although there is a "Rice" function on most of today's electric pressure cookers, they are mostly designed for white and converted rice. When cooking other types of rice, it is best to manually set the machine.

METHOD

White Rice

1. Rinse the rice in a wire mesh strainer until the water is no longer cloudy, about 1 minute under running water. In the inner pot of your electric pressure cooker, stir together the rice, water, and salt. Close and lock the lid, making sure the steam release handle is in the sealing position. Cook on high pressure for 3 minutes.

2. When it is finished, release the pressure naturally for 12 minutes, then turn the steam release handle to venting, releasing any remaining steam. Unlock the lid and open it carefully. Use a fork to rake and fluff the rice before serving.

Brown Rice

1. Rinse the rice in a wire mesh strainer until the water is no longer cloudy, about 1 minute under running water. Stir together the rice, water, and salt in the inner pot of your electric pressure cooker. Close and lock the lid, making sure the steam release handle is in the sealing position. Cook on high pressure for 22 minutes.

2. When it is finished, release the pressure naturally for 10 minutes, then turn the steam release handle to venting, releasing any remaining steam. Unlock the lid and open it carefully. Use a fork to rake and fluff the rice before serving.

Yield: 3 to 4 servings

QUINOA VEGETABLE SALAD WITH LEMON VINAIGRETTE

Gluten Free • Dairy Free • Vegetarian • Vegan • Soy Free • Nut Free • Egg Free

This quinoa salad is packed with fresh seasonal vegetables and lightly dressed with a lemon vinaigrette. It is a great choice all year long, so feel free to use whatever vegetables are fresh and in season. If you are using very firm vegetables, such as cauliflower or broccoli, be sure to par-cook them first to soften them slightly.

INGREDIENTS

For the quinoa

1 cup vegetable stock (page 137) or water

¼ cup (60 ml) water

1 cup (175 g) quinoa, very well rinsed and drained

1 teaspoon kosher or fine sea salt

For the lemon vinaigrette

2 tablespoons (30 ml) freshly squeezed lemon juice

¼ cup (60 ml) extra virgin olive oil

1 teaspoon honey (or to taste)

½ teaspoon fresh thyme leaves

¼ teaspoon kosher or fine sea salt

⅛ teaspoon freshly ground black pepper

For the vegetables

1 tablespoon (15 ml) olive or vegetable oil

2 large carrots, trimmed and finely chopped

2 stalks celery, trimmed and finely chopped

1 large red bell pepper, cored, seeded, and finely chopped

2 tablespoons (20 g) minced red onion

1 cup (150 g) cherry tomatoes, quartered

1 medium cucumber, peeled, seeded, and finely chopped

2 scallions, trimmed and thinly sliced

2 teaspoons (1 g) fresh thyme leaves

Quinoa's natural coating, called saponin, can make it taste bitter or soapy. Rinsing it well under cool running water will get rid of the coating and give you a pleasant-tasting grain to work with. Be sure to agitate the grains with your hands so all sides get equally rinsed.

METHOD

Quinoa

1. Place the stock, water, quinoa, and salt in the inner pot of your electric pressure cooker. Stir and put the lid on the pot. Lock the lid, making sure the steam release handle is in the sealing position. Cook on high pressure for 4 minutes. When the quinoa is finished, let the pressure release naturally for 12 minutes, then turn the steam release handle to venting, releasing any remaining steam. Unlock the lid and open it carefully.

2. Transfer the quinoa to a bowl and set aside. Wipe out the pot and return to the pressure cooker.

Vinaigrette

1. While the quinoa is cooking, make the vinaigrette. In a bowl or jar with a tight lid, whisk together the dressing ingredients until emulsified. If using a jar, you can shake it vigorously to blend. Taste and adjust the seasonings as needed.

Vegetables

1. Press Sauté and heat the oil in the inner pot. Add the carrots, celery, bell pepper, and onion and cook, stirring often, until the onion is softened, about 3 minutes. Press Cancel.

2. Add the sautéed vegetables to the cooked quinoa. Stir in the tomatoes, cucumber, and scallion. Sprinkle the thyme over the top. Dress the salad with about 3 tablespoons (45 ml) of the vinaigrette, tossing to coat the grains and vegetables. Taste and adjust the seasonings, adding more vinaigrette if desired. Place the salad in the refrigerator and chill until ready to serve. The flavors will blend as it rests. Toss again before serving. Can be served cool or at room temperature.

Yield: 4 to 6 servings

SAFFRON RISOTTO

Gluten Free • Dairy-Free Option • Vegetarian • Vegan Option • Soy Free • Nut Free • Egg Free

The key to traditional risotto is constant stirring and adding the broth gradually. This makes it a very time-consuming task and one that can be intimidating to beginning cooks. Today's electric pressure cookers take all the guesswork out of making risotto and you no longer have to stand over the stove stirring while it cooks. You can use any seasonal vegetable in place of the peas if you like, such as asparagus, fava beans, zucchini, and so on. Cut them into small pieces and steam until just tender before adding to the dish.

INGREDIENTS

½ teaspoon saffron threads

3 tablespoons (45 ml) boiling water

1 tablespoon (15 ml) olive or vegetable oil

½ medium onion, finely chopped

1 clove garlic, minced

1½ cups (285 g) Arborio or Carnaroli rice (do not substitute another style of rice)

2 tablespoons (30 ml) dry white wine (optional)

1¾ cups (415 ml) water

2 cups (470 ml) vegetable stock (page 137), divided

½ teaspoon kosher or fine sea salt

¼ teaspoon freshly ground black pepper

2 tablespoons (28 g) unsalted butter or dairy-free/vegan alternative such as Earth Balance

1 teaspoon freshly grated lemon zest (optional)

1 cup (150 g) frozen peas

Grated Parmesan cheese (optional, omit for dairy free and vegan)

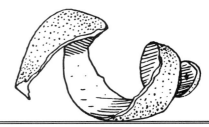

Saffron is a lovely, aromatic, and expensive spice. If you are looking for a less costly alternative, use ½ teaspoon turmeric in its place. Stir it into the rice after you've added the stock. It will add a pretty yellow hue and delicate flavor. It's not as fragrant as saffron, but still delicious.

METHOD

1. In a small bowl, soak the saffron in the hot water.

2. Press Sauté to heat the inner pot of your pressure cooker. Add the oil and heat until shimmering, then stir in the onion and garlic. Cook, stirring often, until the onion has softened slightly, about 4 minutes. Add the rice and stir to coat all the grains with the oil. Pour in the wine and cook until absorbed. Stir in the water, 1½ cups (355 ml) of the stock, the saffron with the soaking water, and the salt and pepper. Stir to make sure no browned bits are stuck on the bottom of the pot. Press Cancel.

3. Close and lock the lid, making sure the handle is in the sealing position. Cook for 4 minutes on high pressure. When it is finished, release the pressure naturally for 8 minutes, then turn the knob to the venting position and quickly release the remaining pressure. Unlock the lid and open it carefully.

4. Stir the rice until smooth and all the liquid has been incorporated. Stir in the butter until melted and the rice is creamy. Stir in the lemon zest and peas. Replace the lid and let the peas steam for 3 minutes. Taste and adjust the seasonings with more salt or pepper if needed. Toss the rice to evenly distribute the peas. If you want a creamier, looser texture, stir in the remaining ½ cup (120 ml) stock.

5. Ladle into bowls, sprinkle each with a little Parmesan cheese, if desired, and serve.

Yield: 4 servings

PLENTIFUL PASTA

Pasta is one of the most missed foods when you have to eat gluten free. Thankfully, there are a number of good-quality products now available for us.

Everyone will have preferences, and you can certainly use what you like, but for consistency while testing the recipes, we settled on a single brand: Barilla gluten-free pasta. We tested a lot of brands while researching this book, and Barilla gluten-free pasta is most readily available in the United States. It gives us consistently good results and holds up to pressure cooking. If it isn't available in your area, you can buy it online. Other brands will likely work but may require different cooking times and may be more fragile.

We found that a blend of rice and corn in gluten-free pasta varieties provides the best of both worlds—good flavor and texture. Gluten-free pastas are more delicate than traditional wheat-based pasta. For this reason, in most cases we cook the pasta first, set it aside while we make the sauce or other steps, then add it back at the end to reheat. This keeps it from getting overcooked and mushy.

A general rule of thumb when cooking gluten-free pasta in the pressure cooker is to cut the recommended cook time in half and then take another minute or two off. Do a controlled pressure release, which means you hold the steam release handle and slowly let the steam out to reduce spewing starchy water all over your kitchen. This stops the cooking more quickly than a natural pressure release. If you are using another brand of pasta, the timing may be different. And different brands may behave differently, so try the recipe as written, and then make adjustments as needed.

Enjoy having pasta again!

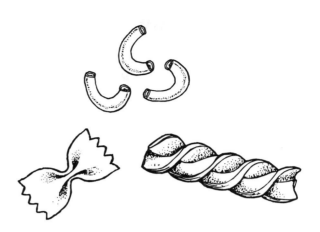

CREAMY MAC AND CHEESE WITH CRISPY BACON

Gluten Free • Vegetarian Option • Soy Free • Nut Free • Egg Free

Mac and cheese is the supreme comfort food, especially beloved by children. Pasta covered with a luscious cheesy sauce is heavenly and something you miss terribly when you can no longer eat gluten. But thanks to the development of good-quality gluten-free pasta, we can make a safe version of our childhood favorite. And if you add it, the bacon lends wonderful flavor and terrific texture on top.

INGREDIENTS

4 slices gluten-free bacon, chopped (optional, replace with 2 tablespoons [30 ml] oil for vegetarian)

½ small onion, grated

3¾ cups (880 ml) water

12 ounces (340 g) uncooked gluten-free elbow macaroni, such as Barilla brand

1½ teaspoons kosher or fine sea salt

1 can (12 ounces, or 340 g) evaporated milk (*not* sweetened condensed) or whole milk

1 teaspoon dry mustard powder

1 teaspoon black pepper

½ teaspoon nutmeg (optional)

24 ounces (672 g) shredded extra-sharp cheddar cheese

8 ounces (227 g) shredded fontina or Monterey Jack cheese

2 ounces (56 g) grated Parmesan cheese

Hot pepper sauce, to taste (optional) (Sriracha brand is gluten free)

METHOD

1. Press Sauté on your electric pressure cooker. When hot, add the bacon to the inner pot and cook, stirring, until crisp. Transfer to a paper towel–lined plate to cool. Remove all but 2 tablespoons (30 ml) of the fat from the inner pot. Add the onion and cook, stirring, until fully softened, about 5 minutes. Press Cancel.

2. Add the water, pasta, and salt to the inner pot. Stir and make sure the pasta is completely covered with the liquid. Close and lock the lid, making certain the steam release handle is in the sealing position. Cook on high pressure for 1 minute.

3. When it is finished, release the pressure naturally for 4 minutes, then slowly vent the remaining pressure by moving the handle between venting and sealing, letting out a little steam at a time. Use a hot pad to protect your hand. When all the steam is released, unlock the lid and open it carefully.

4. Test the pasta; it should be just tender and not too chewy. It will continue cooking as you finish making the dish. If it needs more time, set the lid back on the pressure cooker and let it rest for a few minutes.

5. Stir the milk, mustard powder, pepper, and nutmeg into the cooked pasta. Mix until evenly distributed. Add the cheeses, a little at a time, stirring until melted and creamy before adding more. Add a little hot pepper sauce if desired. If the sauce gets too thick, add ¼ cup (60 ml) hot water or more to thin. Taste and adjust the seasonings if needed. Crumble the bacon and sprinkle on top; serve immediately.

NOTE: The timing for the pasta may change depending on the brand of pasta you use. See page 70 for details.

Yield: About 4 servings

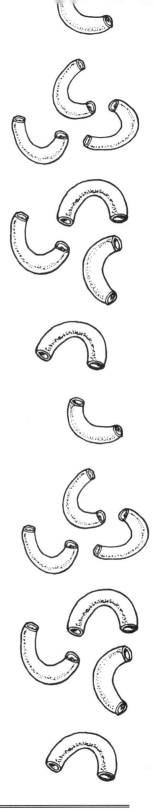

CLASSIC LASAGNA WITH MEAT SAUCE

Gluten Free • Soy Free • Nut Free • Egg Free

Cheesy, meaty, and totally satisfying, this lasagna is a real family favorite. This casserole can be made ahead and frozen to have on hand for busy nights, or you can make a second lasagna if you are feeding a larger crowd. If you don't want to make the meat sauce, you can use a homemade marinara sauce or, if time is tight, your favorite gluten-free jarred pasta sauce works well, too. Some brands we like that have gluten-free varieties include Barilla, Amy's Kitchen, Rao's, Classico, and Muir Glen Organic. Always read the labels to make sure the brand and flavor you choose is gluten free, as manufacturers can change their production practices without notice.

INGREDIENTS

For the meat sauce

1 tablespoon (15 ml) olive or vegetable oil

½ pound (227 g) ground beef

½ pound (227 g) ground pork (*not* sausage)

1 medium onion, finely chopped

2 cloves garlic, minced

2 cups (480 g) gluten-free crushed or strained tomatoes, such Pomi brand

1 tablespoon dried oregano

¼ teaspoon whole fennel seeds

2 teaspoons (12 g) kosher or fine sea salt

½ teaspoon freshly ground black pepper

For the cheese mixture

1 cup (240 g) ricotta cheese

½ cup (50 g) grated Parmesan cheese

2 tablespoons (5 g) chopped fresh basil leaves

2 teaspoons (1 g) dried oregano

½ teaspoon kosher or fine sea salt

½ teaspoon freshly ground black pepper

For assembly

½ (10-ounce, or 283 g) box gluten-free oven-ready lasagna noodles, such as Barilla brand

1½ cups (180 g) shredded mozzarella cheese

¼ cup (25 g) grated Parmesan cheese

Extra chopped basil leaves, for garnish

For the cooking pot

1½ cups (355 ml) water

METHOD

1. Line the bottom of a 7-inch (18 cm) round springform pan or push pan (like you use to make cheesecake) with parchment paper. Line the sides with a strip of parchment. Wrap the bottom of the pan with a sheet of foil to contain any liquids. Set aside.

Meat Sauce

1. Press Sauté on your electric pressure cooker. Add the oil to the inner pot and brown the meats. Use a spoon or flat-edged spatula to break up clumps to get the pieces as small as you can. Add the onion and garlic and cook, stirring, until the onion is softened, about 4 minutes. Stir in the tomatoes, oregano, fennel seeds, salt, and pepper. Simmer for about 5 minutes to blend the flavors. Taste the sauce and add more salt or pepper if needed. Pour into a bowl. Clean the inner pot.

Cheese Mixture

1. In a bowl, stir together the ricotta cheese, Parmesan, basil, oregano, salt, and pepper with a fork until smooth.

Assembly

1. Cover the bottom of the prepared baking pan with some sauce. Break the lasagna noodles to fit in a single layer in the bottom of the pan (see Note). Cover the pasta with more sauce, half of the ricotta mixture, and one-third of the mozzarella. Repeat twice more, each time pressing down gently on the noodle layer to compress slightly. The final layer will be sauce and mozzarella. Sprinkle the top with Parmesan.

2. Spray a piece of foil with nonstick vegetable spray (without flour) and lay it, sprayed side down, on top of the pan. Lightly crimp the edges of the foil to keep the steam out.

3. Pour the water into the bottom of the inner pot. Place a trivet in the bottom. Set the pan on the trivet. Close and lock the lid, making sure the steam release handle is in the sealing position. Cook on high pressure for 24 minutes. When it is finished, release the pressure naturally for 10 minutes, then turn the steam release handle to venting, releasing any remaining steam. Unlock the lid and open it carefully.

4. Lift the pan out of the pot, remove the foil, and insert a knife in several places; it should meet no resistance. Set the pan on a baking sheet. If desired, place under the broiler to brown the cheese on top. Remove from the oven and set aside to rest for 10 minutes before cutting into servings, sprinkling a little chopped basil on top of each piece.

NOTE: Timing for the pasta may change depending on the brand used. See page 70 for details.

Yield: 4 servings

Barilla lasagna noodles fit perfectly into a 7-inch (18 cm) round pan, but if you stack three sheets overlapping like the spokes of a wheel, they may not fully cook through in the center. Break them into smaller pieces and arrange in a jigsaw pattern, slightly overlapping.

VEGETABLE MACARONI SALAD

Gluten Free • Dairy Free • Vegetarian • Nut Free

Pasta salad is standard fare all summer long, showing up on barbecue dinner tables everywhere. With the high-quality gluten-free pastas now available, you can make this easy salad and safely serve it to your entire family. Feel free to use any seasonal vegetables growing in your garden or that you find at your farmers' market to customize this salad.

INGREDIENTS

12 ounces (340 g) gluten-free elbow macaroni, such as Barilla brand

Olive or vegetable oil

2½ teaspoons (15 g) kosher or fine sea salt, divided

½ to ¾ cup (120 to 180 ml) gluten-free Italian salad dressing, such as Girard's Olde Venice Italian Dressing

1 teaspoon sugar (optional)

½ teaspoon freshly ground black pepper

½ teaspoon onion powder

¼ teaspoon ground celery seed

3 scallions, trimmed and finely chopped

2 stalks celery, trimmed and finely chopped

2 red bell peppers, cored, seeded, and finely chopped

1 large cucumber, finely chopped

½ pint (150 g) cherry tomatoes, cut in half

½ cup (50 g) sliced black olives (Lindsay brand is gluten-free)

3 tablespoons (9 g) chopped fresh parsley

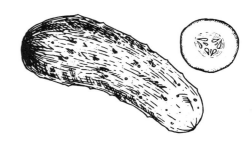

METHOD

1. Place the pasta in the inner pot of your electric pressure cooker. Add fresh water to cover the pasta by 1 inch (2.5 cm). Stir 2 teaspoons (12 g) of the salt into the water and make sure the pasta is not sticking to the bottom of the pot.

2. Close and lock the lid, with the steam release handle in the sealing position. Cook on high pressure for 1 minute. When it is finished, release the pressure naturally for 4 minutes, then turn the steam release handle to venting, releasing remaining steam. When the pressure valve drops, unlock the lid and open it carefully. Pour the pasta into a colander and rinse with cool water to stop the cooking, and then drain thoroughly. Transfer to a large mixing bowl.

3. In a bowl, whisk together the dressing, sugar (if using), ½ teaspoon salt, pepper, onion powder, and celery seed. Pour ½ cup (120 ml) over the pasta and stir in the vegetables and parsley, mixing until evenly distributed and everything is coated with the dressing. Taste and adjust the seasonings, adding more dressing if needed. Store in the refrigerator, covered, until ready to serve.

NOTE: The timing for the pasta may change depending on the brand of pasta you use. See page 70 for details.

Yield: 8 to 10 servings

SHRIMP AND PASTA IN A LEMON CREAM SAUCE

Gluten Free • Soy Free • Nut Free • Egg Free

There is an Italian restaurant in the San Francisco Bay Area that serves pasta in a lemon cream sauce that is always a popular menu item. This recipe's combination of shrimp, dill, lemon, and pasta is a lovely, light yet satisfying meal that would be perfect for luncheons, showers, or brunches. It comes together very quickly and you will have dinner on the table in no time.

INGREDIENTS

For the pasta

12 ounces (340 g) gluten-free penne pasta, such as Barilla brand

1 teaspoon kosher or fine sea salt

Olive oil, for tossing

For the shrimp

1 tablespoon (15 ml) olive or vegetable oil

1 medium shallot, minced

1½ pounds (680 g) raw medium shrimp, peeled and deveined

½ teaspoon minced fresh dill

Kosher or fine sea salt and freshly ground black pepper, to taste

For the lemon cream sauce

3 tablespoons (42 g) unsalted butter

1½ cups (355 ml) heavy cream or evaporated milk

1½ cloves garlic, peeled

2 teaspoons (10 ml) freshly squeezed lemon juice

2 teaspoons (4 g) finely grated lemon zest

1¼ cups (125 g) grated Parmesan cheese, divided

Salt and freshly ground black pepper, to taste

Finely chopped fresh Italian parsley or chives, for garnish

Shrimp come in a variety of sizes, and each will take a different amount of time to cook. You want to cook them in batches so every piece touches the bottom of the pot. When both sides are pink and opaque, remove from the heat and place in a bowl. Continue cooking the remaining shrimp until they are all just done. Cover the bowl and the residual heat will finish cooking them through.

METHOD

Pasta

1. Place the pasta in the inner pot of your pressure cooker. Pour in enough water to cover the pasta by 1 inch (2.5 cm). Stir the pasta to make sure it doesn't stick to the bottom of the pan. Sprinkle the salt in the water. Close and lock the lid, making sure the steam release handle is in the sealing position. Cook on high pressure for 2 minutes.

2. When it is finished, release the pressure naturally for 3 minutes, then do a controlled release by turning the steam release handle to halfway between sealing and venting positions. Protect your hand with a hot pad. When all the steam has been released, press Cancel. Unlock the lid and open it carefully. Pour the pasta into a colander, drain it, and toss with a little oil to keep it from sticking together as it sits. Wipe out the inner pot.

Shrimp

1. Press Sauté and heat the inner pot. Add the oil and when hot, stir in the shallot. Cook for about 1 minute, until just beginning to color. Add the shrimp and dill, tossing to coat with the oil. Cook, stirring often, until the shrimp become opaque and turn pink on both sides, 1 to 2 minutes on each, until just done. Sprinkle lightly with salt and pepper. Use a slotted spoon to scoop the shrimp out of the pot and add to the pasta; cover to keep warm.

Lemon Cream Sauce

1. Add the butter to the inner pot, warming until fully melted. Whisk in the cream, garlic, lemon juice, and zest. Cook until warmed, whisking often to avoid scorching. Discard the garlic. Whisk in 1 cup (100 g) of the Parmesan cheese until smooth. Press Cancel. Taste and adjust the seasonings with salt and pepper if needed.

2. Add the pasta and shrimp to the sauce, tossing to thoroughly coat each piece. Replace the lid and let it rest for a couple of minutes, or until the pasta and shrimp are heated through. Add a splash of water if the sauce gets too thick.

3. To serve, scoop the pasta and shrimp into bowls and sprinkle the top of each serving with 1 tablespoon (6 g) of the remaining Parmesan cheese and a little parsley. Serve hot.

NOTE: The timing for the pasta may change depending on the brand of pasta you use. See page 70 for details.

Yield: 4 servings

PORK TENDERLOIN MARSALA AND PENNE PASTA

Gluten Free • Dairy Free • Soy Free • Nut Free • Egg Free

This Italian dish is usually served with chicken or veal, but we thought it would be fun to try it with a pork tenderloin. The slight sweetness of the wine is a beautiful accompaniment to the pork. The meat is incredibly moist and tender, and the sauce is rich and indulgent. This can be served for special occasions or, because the pork cooks so quickly, for weeknight dinners.

INGREDIENTS

8 ounces (227 g) gluten-free penne pasta

2 teaspoons (12 g) kosher or fine sea salt, plus more to taste

2 tablespoons (30 ml) olive or vegetable oil, divided, plus more for drizzling

1 (about 1½-pound, or 680 g) pork tenderloin

4 slices pancetta or bacon, chopped

1 small onion, finely chopped

1 clove garlic, minced

8 ounces (227 g) cremini or porcini mushrooms, stemmed and halved or quartered

¾ cup (180 ml) sweet Marsala wine or chicken stock (page 136)

¼ cup (60 ml) chicken stock (page 136)

Several sprigs fresh thyme

2 tablespoons (16 g) cornstarch (see page 17 for more information on thickeners)

3 tablespoons (45 ml) cool water

Freshly ground black pepper, as needed

Minced fresh parsley, for garnish

METHOD

1. Place the penne in the inner pot of your electric pressure cooker. Fill the pot with fresh water to cover by 1 inch (2.5 cm). Stir in the salt. Close and lock the lid, making sure the steam release handle is in the sealing position. Cook on high pressure for 2 minutes. When it is finished, release the pressure naturally for 3 minutes, then do a controlled release by holding the handle halfway between the sealing and venting positions. Protect your hand with a hot pad. When all the steam has been released, press Cancel.

2. Unlock the lid and open it carefully. Pour the pasta into a colander and drain. Drizzle with some oil and toss to keep it from sticking together. Set aside and stir occasionally.

3. Press Sauté and heat 1 tablespoon (15 ml) of the oil in the inner pot. When hot, add the pork. Brown for 3 minutes on each side. Transfer the pork to a plate and tent with foil to help keep warm. Add the remaining oil to the pot. Stir in the pancetta and cook until slightly crispy, about 4 minutes, stirring often. Transfer the pancetta to a bowl. Remove all but 2 tablespoons (30 ml) of the fat. Add the onion to the pot and cook for 3 minutes, stirring, until softened. Stir in the garlic, cook for 30 seconds, then stir in the mushrooms. Cook, stirring often, for 2 minutes.

4. Pour in the Marsala wine and chicken stock. Scrape the bottom of the pan to loosen any browned bits. Transfer the pork and its juices back to the pot. Add the cooked pancetta. Close and lock the lid, making sure the steam release handle is in the sealing position.

5. Cook on high pressure for 5 minutes. When it is finished, release the pressure naturally for 7 minutes, then turn the steam release handle to venting, releasing remaining steam. Unlock the lid and open it carefully. Press Cancel. Remove the pork from the pot, check to make sure it has reached at least 140°F in the center with an instant-read thermometer (if it needs more time, return it to the pot and let rest in the heat for a few minutes longer), place on a cutting board, cover, and keep warm.

6. Add the thyme to the pot. In a small bowl, whisk the cornstarch and water together until fully dissolved. Press Sauté and whisk the cornstarch slurry into the cooking liquid in the pot. Cook, whisking constantly, until it thickens. Taste and adjust the seasonings if needed.

7. Stir the pasta into the sauce and return the tenderloin to the pot. Replace the lid and let rest for 1 to 2 minutes to rewarm the pasta. Press Cancel.

8. Cut the pork into thick slices. Divide the pork between plates, add some of the pasta, top with the sauce and mushrooms, sprinkle with the parsley, and serve hot.

NOTE: The timing for the pasta may change depending on the brand of pasta you use. See page 70 for details.

Yield: 3 to 4 servings

MASTERFUL MAIN DISHES

Dinner is one less thing to worry about with your electric pressure cooker. Instead of having to plan ahead and use your oven for hours, you can toss everything in the pressure cooker. The range of dishes you can produce in one pot is simply amazing!

One place where electric pressure cookers really shine is with tough cuts of meat, which normally take hours and hours to become succulent. The technology makes short work of the tenderizing, cutting the time in half or more. The steaming and braising processes leave them luscious and moist without effort. Beef, chicken, fish, pork, ribs, and all types of proteins come out perfectly in your pressure cooker.

Cooking meat in a pressure cooker is wonderful, but who says meat has to be the center of a marvelous meal? Vegetables cooked in a pressure cooker come out just as fantastic. Pressure cooking brings out the natural flavors and delicious complexity of all types of vegetables. It is a fantastic tool for infusing herbs, spices, and other aromatics into your vegetables, legumes, and pulses, thereby creating flavorful, vegetable-focused main dishes. Don't believe us? Try our Vegetable Lasagna (page 98) or Lentil Sloppy Joes (page 100)! These healthy main dishes are not only loaded with flavor, but they can also be on your table in about an hour. With these hearty and satisfying dishes, you'll find plenty of inspiration for your next Meatless Monday!

So whether you are looking for a way to impress guests or simply get a nutritious meal on the table after a long day at work, these are mouthwatering, delicious, gluten-free meals your whole family will enjoy!

CLASSIC WHOLE BAKED CHICKEN

Gluten Free • Dairy Free • Soy Free • Egg Free • Nut Free

This whole baked chicken will make a meal in itself, but you can also cook it on its own and use the meat for any number of other dishes. Try it with our Millet and Chicken Greek Salad (page 62). Be sure to save the chicken carcass to make your own chicken stock (page 136). Serve this chicken as part of a complete meal, with Mashed Potatoes (page 114) or Cheesy Au Gratin Potatoes (page 104).

INGREDIENTS

1 (3- to 5-pound, or 1362 to 2270 g) whole chicken

1 tablespoon (18 g) salt, divided

1 lemon, cut in half

1 onion, cut into quarters

2 teaspoons (4 g) freshly ground pepper

2 teaspoons (4 g) paprika

1 teaspoon dried thyme

1 cup (235 ml) water

Oil or melted unsalted butter (optional, for crisping skin)

Make sure your chicken fits easily inside the inner pot of your pressure cooker. Some whole chickens might be too large.

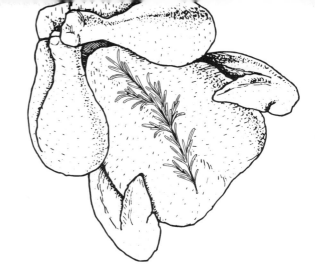

METHOD

1. Remove any giblets or other innards from the cavity of the chicken. Pat dry with a paper towel. Sprinkle 1 teaspoon (6 g) of the salt inside the chicken. Place the cut lemon and onion pieces inside the chicken cavity. Sprinkle the remaining 2 teaspoons (12 g) salt, pepper, paprika, and thyme evenly over the chicken.

2. Put a trivet in the inner pot of your electric pressure cooker and add the water. Place the seasoned chicken, with the breast facing up, on top of the trivet.

3. Close and lock the lid, making sure the steam release knob is in the sealing position. Cook on high pressure for 6 minutes per pound (454 g).

   3-pound (1.4 kg) chicken = 18 minutes

   4-pound (1.8 kg) chicken = 24 minutes

   5-pound (2.3 kg) chicken = 30 minutes

   If your chicken is between weights, add 3 minutes for every half pound (227 g).

   Example: One 4½-pound (2 kg) chicken would equal 27 minutes on high pressure.

4. When the cooking time is finished, allow a natural release for 20 minutes, then move the pressure release knob to the venting position and release any remaining steam. When the float pin drops, unlock the lid and open it carefully.

5. If you like your chicken skin crispy, after removing it from the pot, transfer to a foil-lined baking sheet. Brush with oil or melted butter and place under the broiler for 2 to 4 minutes.

Yield: 4 servings

BBQ BABY BACK RIBS

Gluten Free • Dairy Free • Soy Free • Nut Free • Egg Free

Tender barbecued ribs are a skill that professional grill masters spend years perfecting. Trying to control live fire can be challenging. But if you put those same ribs in an electric pressure cooker, you get perfectly cooked ribs every time with no worry that the weather will interfere and no need to stand watch for hours at the grill. Using a good barbecue sauce, sprinkling with smoked paprika, and broiling at the end help get the flavors close to what you get on the grill with fall-off-the-bone tenderness.

INGREDIENTS

1 (3-pound, or 1.4 kg) rack of baby back ribs

2 tablespoons (30 g) brown sugar

1 tablespoon (6 g) smoked paprika

1 tablespoon (6 g) chili powder (Penzey's and McCormick brands clearly mark their products for allergens)

1 tablespoon (18 g) kosher or fine sea salt

2 teaspoons (1 g) dried thyme leaves

2 teaspoons (2 g) onion powder (*not* onion salt)

1 teaspoon garlic powder (*not* garlic salt)

1 teaspoon freshly ground black pepper

Your favorite gluten-free barbecue sauce (Stubb's brand is gluten free)

For the cooking pot

1¼ cups (295 ml) water

METHOD

1. Lay the ribs bone side up on a baking sheet and remove the membrane covering the surface. Place the trivet in the bottom of the inner pot and pour in the water.

2. In a small bowl, mix together the brown sugar, smoked paprika, chili powder, salt, thyme, onion powder, garlic powder, and pepper. Rub the seasoning mix over all sides of the ribs. Stand the ribs around the edges of the inner pot.

3. Close and lock the lid, making sure the steam release handle is in the sealing position. Cook on high pressure for 17 minutes. When it is finished, release the pressure naturally for 10 minutes, then move the handle to venting and release the remaining steam. Unlock the lid and open it carefully. Press Cancel.

4. Use tongs to transfer the ribs to a clean baking sheet. Preheat the broiler. Lightly brush one side of the ribs with barbecue sauce. Slide the ribs under the broiler for a few minutes until the sauce is bubbling. Flip the pieces over and repeat the broiling, brushing with more sauce. Watch carefully so the ribs don't burn.

5. Serve while hot, passing additional sauce at the table.

Yield: 2 to 3 servings

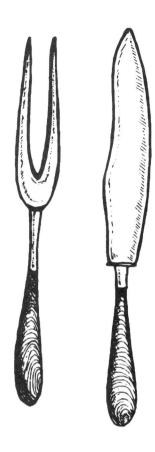

MOM'S OLD-FASHIONED POT ROAST

Gluten Free • Dairy Free • Soy Free • Nut Free • Egg Free

There is nothing that smells better when it is cooking than old-fashioned pot roast, packed with tender beef, potatoes, and carrots. With today's pressure cookers, we can have this dinner on the table in much less time than it takes to roast it in the oven, with all the flavor and tenderness we love. If you like, you can serve this over Mashed Potatoes (page 114).

INGREDIENTS

1 (3-pound, or 1.4 kg) boneless chuck roast

¾ teaspoon kosher or fine sea salt

½ teaspoon freshly ground black pepper

2 tablespoons (30 ml) olive oil

2 cups (470 ml) gluten-free beef stock (page 134)

½ cup (120 ml) dry red wine or water

1 large onion, coarsely chopped

1 clove garlic, minced

2 bay leaves

1 teaspoon dried rosemary leaves

3 large russet potatoes, peeled and cut into large chunks

4 large carrots, trimmed and cut into large chunks

¼ cup (60 ml) cool water

2 tablespoons (16 g) cornstarch or potato starch

⅓ cup (50 g) frozen peas (optional)

2 tablespoons (6 g) finely chopped fresh parsley

Some people like tomato in their pot roast cooking liquid. If you want, you can whisk 2 tablespoons (30 g) tomato paste concentrate into the stock before adding the aromatics and seasonings.

METHOD

1. Pat the meat dry with paper towels and season with the salt and pepper. Press Sauté and pour the oil into the inner pot. When the oil is shimmering, add the meat and brown on both sides, about 5 minutes per side. Add the stock and wine, stirring to release any browned bits on the bottom of the pan. Stir in the onion, garlic, bay leaves, and rosemary. Press Cancel.

2. Close and lock the lid, making sure the steam release handle is in the sealing position. Cook on high pressure for 70 minutes. When it is finished, allow the pot to naturally release the pressure for 12 minutes, then turn the steam release handle to venting, releasing any remaining steam. Unlock the lid and open it carefully.

3. Quickly add the potatoes and carrots to the pot, replace the lid, set the steam release handle to sealing, bring back to pressure, and cook on high pressure for 3 minutes. Move the handle to venting and release the steam. Unlock the lid and open it carefully.

4. Using a slotted spoon and tongs, transfer the meat and vegetables to a platter. Discard the bay leaves and tent with foil to keep warm. Press Cancel.

5. In a small bowl, whisk together the water and cornstarch. While whisking, slowly pour the cornstarch slurry into the cooking liquid until fully blended. Press Sauté and bring the liquid in the pot to a boil, whisking constantly. Cook until thickened, about 1 minute, then taste and adjust the seasonings if needed. Press Cancel.

6. Stir in the peas, then return the meat and vegetables to the pot, stirring into the sauce. Place the lid on the pot and let sit for 4 minutes, or until peas are thawed and the meat is heated through. Scoop the meat and vegetables into bowls with some of the sauce, sprinkle with the chopped parsley, and serve.

Yield: 4 to 6 servings

SOUTHWESTERN MEATLOAF

Gluten Free • Dairy Free • Soy Free • Nut Free • Egg Free

Most meatloaf recipes have eggs and bread crumbs in them as binders. I have found that you don't need either. The loaf will hold together without the binders, and that gives us a gluten-free dinner! By sautéing the vegetables, they soften enough to easily be mixed into the ground meat. Just be sure to chop them finely or it will be harder to make the loaf hold together. Loaded with the flavors of the American Southwest, this is not your mother's meatloaf. Serve with Mashed Potatoes (page 114), if you like.

INGREDIENTS

1 tablespoon (15 ml) olive or vegetable oil

½ large onion, very finely chopped

2 stalks celery, very finely chopped

2 carrots, very finely chopped

1 red bell pepper, cored, seeded, and very finely chopped

1 pound (454 g) lean ground beef

1 tablespoon (15 ml) Worcestershire sauce (Lea & Perrins brand is gluten free)

2 teaspoons (1 g) chopped fresh cilantro

2 teaspoons (4 g) gluten-free ancho chile powder or chili powder

1 teaspoon kosher or fine sea salt

1 teaspoon ground cumin

½ teaspoon freshly ground black pepper

¼ teaspoon garlic powder (*not* garlic salt)

¼ cup (60 ml) barbecue sauce (Stubb's brand is gluten free)

1 cup (60 ml) water

If you have picky eaters who won't touch vegetables, you can puree them with a little water or tomato sauce after cooking and mix the puree into the meat. They will eat their vegetables without ever knowing it!

METHOD

1. Press Sauté on your electric pressure cooker. When the inner pot is hot, add the oil. Add the onion, celery, carrots, and pepper and cook, stirring often, until the onion has softened, 3 to 5 minutes. Press Cancel. Remove the inner pot from the machine and set aside to cool slightly.

2. In a bowl, combine the meat with the Worcestershire and seasonings, mixing by hand until evenly seasoned. Add the cooled vegetables and fold in. When evenly distributed, pat the meat into a mounded disk about 6 inches (15 cm) in diameter and place in a 7-inch (18 cm) round baking pan. Brush the barbecue sauce over the top of the loaf. Cover the pan with foil. Wipe out the inner pot.

3. Place a trivet in the bottom of the inner pot and pour in the water. Set the meatloaf onto a rack with handles or a sling (see page 15) and lower onto the trivet. Close and lock the lid, making sure the steam release handle is in the sealing position. Cook on high pressure for 22 minutes, or until an instant-read thermometer registers at least 160°F (71°C) when inserted into the center of the meatloaf.

4. When it is finished, release the pressure naturally for 8 minutes, then release the rest of the pressure by moving the handle to the venting position. Unlock the lid and open it carefully.

5. Lift the sling out of the inner pot, carefully remove the foil from the pan, and transfer the meatloaf to a baking sheet. If desired, you can slide it under the broiler for a few minutes to brown the top.

6. Cut into slices to serve and pass additional barbecue sauce at the table.

Yield: 4 servings

ROAST TURKEY BREAST WITH EASY GRAVY

Gluten Free • Soy Free • Nut Free • Egg Free

This easy roast turkey can be on your dinner table in just over an hour. As the turkey cooks, it's creating the base for a flavorful gravy that comes together quickly without any flour, making it a completely gluten-free meal. This meal is fancy enough to serve for the holidays or a special Sunday dinner, but it is also easy enough to make during the week if you're in the mood for some solid comfort food. Searing the turkey before you cook it will give it a nice golden brown color and a deeper flavor! Serve with Mashed Potatoes (page 114).

INGREDIENTS

For the turkey

3 tablespoons (45 ml) olive or vegetable oil, divided

1 (4- to 5-pound, or 1.8 to 2.3 kg) turkey breast (Jenni-O brand is gluten free)

3 tablespoons (6 g) chopped fresh thyme

2 tablespoons (6 g) chopped fresh rosemary

2 teaspoons (12 g) salt

1 tablespoon (6 g) freshly cracked black pepper

5 cloves garlic, minced

2 tablespoons (28 g) unsalted butter

½ medium onion, sliced

1 cup (235 ml) gluten-free chicken stock (page 136)

For the gravy

3 tablespoons (42 g) unsalted butter

3 tablespoons (24 g) cornstarch or potato starch

½ cup (120 ml) half-and-half

Salt and pepper to taste

If you're a fan of crispier skin, place your cooked turkey on a sheet pan under the broiler for about 5 minutes while you're making the gravy. Watch it carefully so it doesn't get too brown.

METHOD

Turkey

1. Drizzle 1 tablespoon (15 ml) of the oil all over the turkey breast. Coat with the thyme, rosemary, salt, pepper, and minced garlic.

2. Press Sauté on your electric pressure cooker. When the inner pot is hot, add the 2 tablespoons (28 g) butter and the remaining 2 tablespoons (30 ml) olive oil. When the butter is melted, add the turkey breast and sear on all sides, about 8 minutes. When the turkey is golden brown, transfer to a plate or a cutting board.

3. In the remaining turkey fat, add the onion and sauté until softened, 3 to 4 minutes. Press Cancel.

4. Add the broth to the pot. Stir to scrape up any browned bits. Place the trivet in the bottom of the inner pot, on top of the onions. Place the browned turkey on top of the trivet.

5. Close and lock the lid, making sure the steam release knob is in the sealing position. Cook on high pressure for 35 minutes. When the turkey is finished cooking, allow a 15-minute natural release, then move the handle to venting and release any remaining steam. When the float pin drops, unlock the lid and open it carefully.

6. Check your turkey with an instant-read thermometer to ensure it is at least 165°F (74°C). If it is not, return the lid and cook at high pressure for an additional 4 to 5 minutes with a 10-minute natural release. Once your turkey is at a safe 165°F (74°C), remove it from the pressure cooker and transfer it to a cutting board. Cover the turkey breast with aluminum foil and let it rest for 15 minutes before slicing.

Gravy

1. After removing the turkey breast from the pressure cooker, press Sauté. Add the 3 tablespoons (42 g) butter to the liquid at the bottom of the pan. Cook until the butter is melted.

2. In a small bowl, whisk together the cornstarch and 3 tablespoons (45 ml) of the cooking liquid from the pot to form a slurry. Add the slurry back to the pot and continue to whisk until the gravy thickens, about 2 minutes. Add the half-and-half and stir until just heated through. Add salt and pepper to taste.

3. Pour the gravy over the sliced turkey breast and serve.

Yield: 8 servings

SHRIMP AND GRITS

Gluten Free • Nut Free • Soy Free

This recipe is an easy way to impress guests or to serve as a quick weeknight dinner. It is so rich and decadent, yet it's still good old-fashioned, down-home casual fare. Add more hot sauce than is listed here if you like your grits with a bit more kick. Making the grits and the sauce together not only saves time but also frees you for other things, like setting the table or helping your kids with homework while dinner cooks.

INGREDIENTS

For the shrimp

1 pound (454 g) shrimp, peeled and deveined

1 tablespoon (3 g) Old Bay Seasoning (Old Bay is gluten free)

3 slices smoked bacon, diced (Applegate Farms has gluten-free bacon)

1 medium yellow onion, chopped

1 red or green bell pepper, cored, seeded, and chopped

3 cloves garlic, minced

½ cup (120 ml) gluten-free chicken stock (page 136)

1 (14.5-ounce, or 406 g) can diced tomatoes

2 tablespoons (30 ml) freshly squeezed lemon juice

½ teaspoon Tabasco or hot sauce, to taste

½ teaspoon salt

½ teaspoon fresh cracked black pepper

¼ cup (60 ml) heavy cream

¼ cup (25 g) thinly sliced scallion, green parts only

For the grits

¾ cup (105 g) grits (such as Bob's Red Mill gluten-free coarse corn grits)

1½ cups (355 ml) whole milk

1½ cups (355 ml) water

½ teaspoon salt

½ teaspoon fresh cracked black pepper

2 tablespoons (28 g) unsalted butter

METHOD

Shrimp

1. Pat the shrimp dry, sprinkle with the Old Bay Seasoning, and set aside.

2. Press Sauté on your electric pressure cooker. When the inner pot is hot, add the diced bacon and cook until crisp, 3 to 5 minutes. Transfer the bacon to a paper towel–lined plate, but leave the bacon drippings in the pot. Add the onion and bell pepper to the pot and cook until the onion is soft and translucent, 2 to 3 minutes. Add the garlic and cook for an additional 30 seconds, until fragrant.

3. Add the chicken stock to the pot, stirring well to release any browned bits from the bottom. Add the tomatoes and their juices, lemon juice, hot sauce, salt, and pepper. Stir to combine. Press Cancel.

4. Place a trivet in the pot. Make sure the base of the trivet sits above the sauce.

Grits

1. In a medium glass or stainless steel bowl that will fit inside your pressure cooker, whisk together the grits, milk, water, salt, and pepper. Cover the bowl with aluminum foil, crimping the edges to seal. Using a foil sling (see page 15), carefully place the bowl on the trivet inside the inner pot.

2. Close and lock the lid, making sure the steam release handle is in the sealing position. Cook on high pressure for 10 minutes. Allow a natural pressure release for 15 minutes, then turn the knob to the venting position, releasing any remaining steam. When the float pin drops, unlock the lid and open it carefully. Remove the bowl with the grits and set aside.

3. Remove the trivet from the pot using a pair of tongs. Add the seasoned shrimp to the pot. Close and lock the lid again to allow the shrimp to finish cooking in the residual heat, 6 to 8 minutes.

4. While the shrimp are cooking, add the butter to the grits and whisk until the butter is completely melted and the mixture is creamy.

5. Open the pressure cooker and gently stir the shrimp. Press Cancel. Press Sauté, then stir the cream into the shrimp mixture. Heat until warmed through, stirring constantly. Do not boil the sauce.

6. Spoon the grits into individual serving dishes, then top with the shrimp and sauce. Garnish with the scallions and reserved bacon.

Yield: 4 servings

MARVELOUS MEATBALL STROGANOFF

Gluten Free • Nut Free

This dish has a kid-friendly twist by using turkey meatballs instead of flank steak. The meatballs are a fun and different addition and don't require any flour or bread crumbs as a binder. In a healthy twist, it doesn't use canned soup to achieve the traditional deep, rich flavor, bypassing an ingredient that usually has gluten in it. Serve over Mashed Potatoes (page 114) or your favorite gluten-free noodles.

INGREDIENTS

1 pound (454 g) ground turkey (Jennie-O brand is gluten free)

1 egg

2 tablespoons (30 ml) milk

1 teaspoon onion powder

¼ cup (12 g) chopped fresh parsley, plus more for garnish

1 tablespoon (2 g) fresh thyme leaves

1 teaspoon salt

1 teaspoon freshly ground black pepper

2 tablespoons (30 ml) olive oil

1 medium onion, thinly sliced

3 cloves garlic, minced

2½ cups (588 ml) gluten-free beef stock (page 134), divided

½ cup (120 g) sour cream

2 tablespoons (16 g) potato starch

1 teaspoon smoked paprika

1 tablespoon (15 g) tomato paste

1 tablespoon (6 g) beef bouillon granules (Herb-Ox brand is gluten free)

½ teaspoon Worcestershire sauce (Lee & Perrins brand is gluten free)

½ pound (227 g) sliced button mushrooms

2 tablespoons (16 g) cornstarch

2 tablespoons (30 ml) cold water

METHOD

1. In a large bowl, combine the ground turkey, egg, milk, onion powder, parsley, thyme, salt, and pepper until just combined. Shape into 20 (1-inch, or 2.5 cm) meatballs.

2. Press Sauté on your electric pressure cooker. When the inner pot is hot, add the oil and brown the meatballs, 2 to 3 minutes per side. Once the meatballs are brown, transfer them to a serving dish and set aside.

3. Add the sliced onion to the pot and cook until just tender, 3 to 4 minutes. Add the garlic and cook for an additional 30 seconds, until fragrant. Add 1 cup (235 ml) of the beef stock to the pan and scrape up any browned bits on the bottom of the pot.

4. In a small bowl, combine the remaining 1½ cups (353 ml) beef stock, sour cream, potato starch, paprika, tomato paste, bouillon, and Worcestershire sauce. Stir until well combined. Add to the onion mixture already in the pan. Return the meatballs to the pot, submerging them completely in the sauce.

5. Close and lock the lid, making sure the steam release handle is in the sealing position. Cook on high pressure for 10 minutes. When the cooking time is finished, turn off your pressure cooker and allow a natural release of 20 minutes, or until the float pin drops. When the float pin has dropped, unlock the lid and open it carefully.

6. Add the sliced mushrooms to the pot. Stir well, then close the lid and let sit for 3 minutes to soften the mushrooms.

7. In a small bowl, mix the cornstarch and cold water together to create a slurry. Press Sauté or Browning on your electric pressure cooker again and allow the sauce to heat up. When the sauce is bubbling, add the cornstarch mixture to the pot and whisk constantly for 2 minutes, or until the sauce thickens.

8. Sprinkle with additional parsley, if desired.

Yield: 5 servings (4 meatballs each)

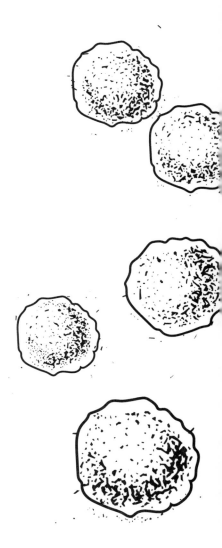

VEGETABLE LASAGNA

Gluten Free • Vegetarian • Soy Free • Nut Free

This vegetable lasagna is so hearty, you won't miss the meat. The layers of vegetables and noodles come together perfectly in the pressure cooker. It's stuffed with not only plenty of vegetables but also three different cheeses, so even your favorite meat-eaters are going to love it. Serve with a nice green salad and you've got a complete meal in under an hour! For a crisp top, put the finished lasagna under the broiler for a few minutes to brown. Be sure to watch it carefully so it doesn't burn.

INGREDIENTS

1 tablespoon (15 ml) olive oil

1 medium onion, diced

4 cloves garlic, minced

1 teaspoon red pepper flakes

2 cups (140 g) sliced button mushrooms

1 cup (120 g) finely diced carrot

1 cup (150 g) finely diced red bell pepper

1½ cups (355 ml) water

1 cup (240 g) low-fat ricotta cheese or small-curd cottage cheese

1½ cups (180 g) part-skim mozzarella cheese, divided

1 cup (100 g) grated Parmesan cheese, divided

1 egg

1 tablespoon (6 g) dried oregano

1 teaspoon dried parsley

6 to 9 no-boil, oven-ready, gluten-free lasagna noodles, such as Barilla brand (see Note)

3 cups (750 g) your favorite gluten-free marinara sauce

¼ cup (10 g) chopped fresh basil leaves

2 medium zucchini, thinly sliced lengthwise

The pan you use for this recipe should be at least 3 inches (7.6 cm) deep. Anything less won't fit all the delicious vegetable and cheese layers.

METHOD

1. Press Sauté on your electric pressure cooker. When the inner pot is hot, add the oil and onion. Cook for 2 to 3 minutes, or until the onion begins to soften. Add the garlic and red pepper flakes and cook for an additional 30 seconds, until the garlic is fragrant.

2. Add the mushrooms, carrot, and bell pepper to the pot. Cook for another 2 minutes. Remove the sautéed vegetables to a medium bowl. Drain any excess liquids. Set aside.

3. Rinse your pot and dry well, inside and out. Return the inner pot to the body of your pressure cooker. Place a trivet in the bottom of the pot and add the water. Spray a 7 x 3-inch (18 x 7.6 cm) push pan or round cake pan with nonstick cooking spray.

4. In a small bowl, combine the ricotta cheese, 1 cup (120 g) of the mozzarella cheese, ½ cup (50 g) of the Parmesan cheese, egg, oregano, and parsley. Set aside.

5. Break 3 pasta pieces and arrange them evenly in the bottom of the pan. A little bit of overlap is fine. Spread 1 cup (250 g) of the marinara sauce over the noodles. Layer half of the chopped basil over the sauce. Add half of the zucchini slices and spread half of the drained vegetable mixture over the slices. Spread half of the cheese mixture over the vegetables, spreading as evenly as possible.

6. Repeat with another layer of pasta, sauce, basil, zucchini, vegetables, and cheese. Top with the remaining 3 pasta sheets and remaining 1 cup (250 g) tomato sauce. Sprinkle the remaining ½ cup (60 g) mozzarella and remaining ½ cup (50 g) Parmesan cheese on top.

7. Cover the pan with aluminum foil, crimping the edges to seal. Using a foil sling (see page 15), lower the lasagna pan onto the trivet.

8. Close and lock the lid, making sure the steam release knob is in the sealing position. Cook on high pressure for 20 minutes. When the cook time is finished, allow a 10-minute natural release, then turn the knob to the venting position, releasing any remaining steam. When the float pin drops, unlock the lid and open it carefully.

9. Allow the lasagna to sit for a few minutes to set, then carefully remove it from the pan.

NOTES: The timing for the pasta may change depending on the brand of pasta you use. See page 70 for details.

The Barilla lasagna noodles fit perfectly into a 7-inch (18 cm) round pan, but if you stack 3 sheets overlapping like the spokes of a wheel, they may not fully cook through in the center. Break them into smaller pieces and arrange in a jigsaw pattern, slightly overlapping.

Yield: 4 servings

LENTIL SLOPPY JOES

Gluten Free • Dairy Free • Nut Free • Vegetarian

When you need something hearty to feed a crowd, this is it! Grab a fork on the way, because these lentil sloppy Joes are definitely sloppy! Smoky, tender, slightly spicy, with a hint of sweetness and a rich tomato flavor, this recipe is quick to put together and sure to bring back memories of childhood dinners. Serve these with French fries or a green salad. If you want to skip the bread altogether, this mixture is great in lettuce cups or served over steamed rice.

INGREDIENTS

1 tablespoon (15 ml) vegetable oil

1 large yellow onion, diced

5 cloves garlic, minced

2 carrots, peeled and diced small

1 green bell pepper, cored, seeded, and diced

2 cups (380 g) brown or green lentils, rinsed

1 cup (235 ml) water or gluten-free vegetable stock (page 137)

1 (14.5-ounce, or 406 g) can fire-roasted diced tomatoes (including juices)

1 (15-ounce, or 420 g) can tomato sauce

3 tablespoons (45 g) tomato paste

2 to 3 tablespoons (30 to 45 g) brown sugar (to taste)

2 tablespoons (30 ml) Worcestershire sauce (Lea & Perrins brand is gluten free)

2 teaspoons (4 g) ground cumin

1 tablespoon (6 g) chili powder

2 teaspoons (4 g) smoked paprika

4 gluten-free hamburger buns, such as Udi's, for serving

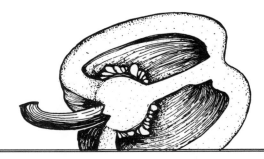

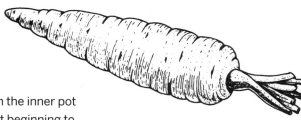

METHOD

1. Press Sauté on your electric pressure cooker. When the inner pot is hot, add the oil. Add the onion and sauté until just beginning to soften, 3 minutes. Add the garlic and cook for an additional 30 seconds, until fragrant.

2. Add all the remaining ingredients (except the buns) to the pot and stir well.

3. Close and lock the lid, making sure the steam release knob is in the sealing position. Cook on high pressure for 15 minutes. When the cook time is finished, allow a full natural pressure release (about 20 minutes). When the float pin has dropped, unlock the lid and open it carefully.

4. Taste and adjust the seasonings as needed. Add more chili powder or cumin for spice and smokiness, brown sugar for a sweeter sloppy Joe, or a little more Worcestershire for deeper flavor.

Yield: 4 servings

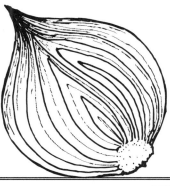

SENSATIONAL SIDE DISHES

The perfect accompaniment to your favorite main dishes, these sensational sides will have you singing with joy over how simple they are to make. There is no need to take up precious space in the oven when you can utilize your pressure cooker to do the work for you. These sides include gluten-free versions of many family favorites, so you can balance dinner with something wholesome and comforting.

Did you know that most corn bread recipes have wheat flour in them? It is another sneaky place you will find gluten. We've given you a savory version (page 110), as well as a corn bread stuffing recipe that is perfect for your holiday turkey (page 112).

To make sure you have everything you need for a perfect Thanksgiving feast or Christmas dinner, we've shared our favorite classic side dishes that everyone asks for each year, complete with Green Bean Casserole with Fried Onions (page 108) and Cheesy Au Gratin Potatoes (page 104). You're all set for a great holiday season, but we hope you and your family enjoy every one of these delightful recipes all year long!

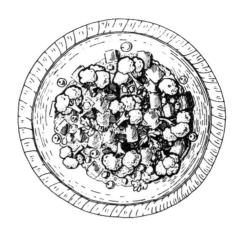

CHEESY AU GRATIN POTATOES

Gluten Free • Nut Free • Soy Free • Vegetarian

Always at home on any dinner table, these versatile cheesy potatoes are the perfect side dish for any number of entrées. The combination of two different cheeses and sour cream to create a silky cheese sauce, along with a crunchy topping of gluten-free panko bread crumbs, creates a delectable side dish everyone will love. Watch the potatoes carefully in the broiler so the topping doesn't get too brown. Use these cheesy potatoes as an accompaniment to our Roast Turkey Breast with Easy Gravy (page 92), Classic Whole Baked Chicken (page 84), or BBQ Baby Back Ribs (page 86).

INGREDIENTS

2 tablespoons (28 g) unsalted butter

1 medium onion, chopped

2 cloves garlic, minced

1 cup (235 ml) gluten-free vegetable stock (page 137)

½ teaspoon salt

¼ teaspoon freshly cracked black pepper

6 medium russet potatoes, peeled and sliced ⅛ inch (3 mm) thick

1 cup (55 g) gluten-free panko bread crumbs

3 tablespoons (45 ml) melted unsalted butter

½ cup (120 g) sour cream

½ cup (60 g) shredded mild cheddar cheese

½ cup (60 g) shredded Gruyère cheese

Switch things up by experimenting with different cheese combinations for the sauce. Sharp cheddar, Parmesan, Swiss, or pepper Jack would all be delicious in this recipe. Keep the portions the same and you'll have an endless variety of potato dishes to go with any meal!

METHOD

1. Press Sauté or Browning on your electric pressure cooker. When the inner pot is hot, add the 2 tablespoons (28 g) butter. When the butter is melted, add the onion and cook, stirring occasionally, until tender, about 5 minutes. Add the garlic and cook for an additional 30 seconds, until fragrant. Add the stock, salt, and pepper, scraping up any browned bits from the bottom of the pot.

2. Add a steamer basket to the bottom of your pot over the onion and garlic mixture. Placed the sliced potatoes in the basket. Close and lock the lid, making sure the steam release valve is in the sealing position. Cook on high pressure for 7 minutes.

3. While the potatoes are cooking, preheat your broiler and grease a 9 x 13-inch (23 x 33 cm) casserole dish. In a small bowl, combine the panko bread crumbs with the 3 tablespoons (45 ml) melted butter. Stir to coat all the bread crumbs. Set aside.

4. When the potatoes are finished cooking, use the quick release method by opening the release handle and venting all the steam. When the float pin drops, unlock the lid and open it carefully.

5. Remove the potatoes and the steamer basket from the pressure cooker. Place the potatoes into the prepared casserole dish. While the pot is still hot, add the sour cream and both of the cheeses to the cooking liquid in the pressure cooker. Stir until the cheese is completely melted and the mixture is smooth.

6. Carefully pour the cheese sauce over the cooked potatoes in the dish and stir gently to combine. Top the potatoes with the bread crumbs mixture. Place under the broiler for 5 to 6 minutes, or until the topping is a nice golden brown.

Yield: 6 servings

"HITS THE SPOT" BRUSSELS SPROUTS

Gluten Free • Vegetarian Option • Soy Free

These family-favorite Brussels sprouts really hit the spot when the weather cools down and fall is in the air. The salty-sweet combination of bacon paired with the bright green sprouts and the tart apples and cranberries is the quintessential holiday dish. We can't get enough of the creamy cheese and crunchy hazelnuts on top either! It's flavorful comfort food that pairs perfectly with pork and turkey dishes.

INGREDIENTS

2 tablespoons (30 ml) olive or vegetable oil

6 strips of gluten-free bacon, chopped (optional)

⅓ cup (79 ml) apple cider vinegar (Braggs brand is gluten free)

¼ cup (60 ml) maple syrup

1 teaspoon ground ginger

1 teaspoon salt

1 teaspoon coarsely ground pepper

2 pounds (907 g) fresh Brussels sprouts, trimmed and cut in half

2 large Fuji apples, peeled, cored, and diced

¼ cup (30 g) dried cranberries

½ cup (58 g) chopped hazelnuts, toasted

¼ cup (38 g) crumbled goat cheese

METHOD

1. Press Sauté on your electric pressure cooker. When the inner pot is hot, add the oil. Add the chopped bacon and cook until crisp and crumbly. Move the bacon to a paper towel–lined plate, but leave the drippings in the pan. Set the bacon aside. Press Cancel.

2. Add the cider vinegar, maple syrup, ginger, salt, and pepper to the pot and whisk to combine with bacon drippings. Add the Brussels sprouts, apples, and dried cranberries, tossing well to coat.

3. Close and lock the lid, making sure the steam release knob is closed in the sealing position. Cook on high pressure for 1 minute. When it is finished, use a quick release by opening the release knob and venting the steam. When the float pin drops, unlock the lid and open it carefully.

4. Serve the Brussels sprouts sprinkled with the reserved bacon, hazelnuts, and crumbled goat cheese.

Yield: 6 servings

GREEN BEAN CASSEROLE WITH FRIED ONIONS

Gluten Free • Soy Free • Nut Free

Everyone's favorite holiday dish, this green bean casserole has a creamy mushroom sauce wrapped around tender green beans and is made completely from scratch, without using any canned soup, which could contain hidden gluten. The fried onion topping uses tapioca flour to create a thin, crispy breading that adds to the classic flavor of this dish. It is decadent enough to satisfy everyone at your dinner table, whether they are gluten free or not.

INGREDIENTS

For the green beans

2 tablespoons (28 g) unsalted butter

1 large onion, halved and thinly sliced

5 cloves garlic, finely diced

1 pound (454 g) button mushrooms, sliced

1 teaspoon salt

1½ pounds (680 g) fresh green beans

¼ teaspoon ground nutmeg

½ teaspoon red pepper flakes

1 cup (235 ml) gluten-free vegetable stock (page 137)

3 tablespoons (34 g) diced roasted red bell peppers

½ cup (120 ml) heavy cream

2 tablespoons (30 ml) cold water (optional)

2 tablespoons (16 g) cornstarch (optional)

For the fried onion topping

Vegetable oil, for frying

3 tablespoons (24 g) tapioca flour

1 teaspoon salt

¼ teaspoon black pepper

1 medium onion, thinly sliced into rings

METHOD

Green Beans

1. Press Sauté or Browning on your electric pressure cooker. When the inner pot is hot, add the butter. When the butter has melted, add the onion and cook for 5 minutes, or until softened and just beginning to brown. Add the garlic and cook for an additional 30 seconds, until fragrant.

2. Add the sliced mushrooms to the onions, sprinkle with the salt, and cook for 3 minutes, stirring occasionally. Press Cancel while you prepare the green beans.

3. Rinse the green beans under cold water and trim the ends. If the green beans are too long, cut them in half so they will fit into your pressure cooker. Add the green beans, nutmeg, red pepper flakes, and vegetable stock to the mushrooms and onions in the pot. Stir to combine.

4. Close and lock the lid, making sure the steam release knob is in the sealing position. Cook on high pressure for 1 minute. When it is finished, use a quick release by opening the release knob and venting all the steam. When the float pin drops, unlock the lid and open it carefully.

5. Add the roasted red bell peppers and heavy cream to the green beans. Stir until well combined. If the mixture is too thin for your liking, make a slurry by mixing the cold water and cornstarch in a small bowl and whisking until the mixture is smooth. Add the slurry to the beans and stir until it thickens. Press Cancel, but return the lid to keep the beans warm. Spray an 8-inch (20.3 cm) casserole dish with nonstick cooking spray and set aside.

Fried Onion Topping

1. In a medium saucepan, heat 1 inch (2.5 cm) of vegetable oil to 375°F (190°C).

2. In a bowl, combine the tapioca flour, salt, and pepper. Stir gently to combine. Add the thinly sliced onions and toss with your hands until the onion is well coated with flour.

3. Very gently shake any excess flour off the onion rings and carefully place a few at a time into the hot oil. Fry the onions in small batches until golden brown and crispy. When they are done, remove the onions from the oil with a slotted spoon and drain them on a paper towel–lined plate.

4. When all the onions are done cooking, open the lid of your pressure cooker and transfer the green bean mixture to the prepared casserole dish. Spread the fried onions over the green beans and place the dish under the broiler for 3 to 4 minutes, until heated through and crispy on top.

Yield: 6 servings

SAVORY CORN BREAD

Gluten Free • Dairy-Free Option • Soy Free • Nut Free

Do you miss having bread stuffing during the holidays? Here is a way to have a delicious gluten-free stuffing on your table! Make this savory corn bread a few days ahead so it can be transformed into stuffing or, if you wish, make it fresh as a side dish for our Pumpkin Black Bean Chili (page 52). It will be delicious either way!

INGREDIENTS

1 cup (120 g) brown rice flour (Authentic Foods brand is gluten free and not gritty)

½ cup (60 g) sorghum flour (Bob's Red Mill brand is gluten free)

¾ cup (105 g) plus 2 tablespoons (18 g) medium-grind gluten-free cornmeal, divided

2 teaspoons (5 g) baking powder

½ teaspoon salt

½ teaspoon onion powder

½ teaspoon garlic powder

1 teaspoon psyllium husk powder or ½ teaspoon xanthan gum

1 teaspoon finely chopped fresh thyme

¼ cup (56 g) unsalted butter or dairy-free butter such as Earth Balance

1 cup (235 ml) milk or dairy-free milk

1 egg, lightly beaten

1 cup (235 ml) water

METHOD

1. Spray a 7 x 3-inch (18 x 7.6 cm) cake pan with nonstick cooking spray, then dust with 2 tablespoons (18 g) of the cornmeal. Set aside.

2. In a large mixing bowl, combine the two flours, remaining ¾ cup (105 g) cornmeal, baking powder, salt, onion and garlic powders, psyllium husk powder, and thyme. Whisk together until thoroughly blended.

3. In a microwave-safe bowl, melt the butter and whisk into the flour mixture; add the milk and beaten egg. Whisk to combine all of the ingredients and stir until smooth.

4. Pour into the prepared baking pan and tap lightly on the counter to release any air bubbles. Spray a square of aluminum foil with nonstick cooking spray and place (sprayed side down) over the corn bread mixture.

5. Add the water to the inner pot of your pressure cooker. Place a trivet in the pot. Using a foil sling (see page 15), carefully lower the covered cake pan into the pot on top of the trivet.

6. Close and lock the lid, making sure the steam release knob is in the sealing position. Cook on high pressure for 35 minutes. When the cook time is finished, do a quick pressure release by carefully moving the sealing knob to venting and allowing all the steam to escape. When the float pin drops, unlock the lid and open it carefully.

7. Remove the corn bread from the pot and place on a cooling rack. Remove the foil from the top and let the corn bread cool to room temperature.

Yield: 4 servings

CORN BREAD STUFFING

Gluten Free • Dairy-Free Option • Soy Free

Thanksgiving and other family gatherings are all about abundance, and with this recipe everyone at your table can enjoy homemade stuffing. Full of apples, cranberries, and nuts, it is the perfect accompaniment to your turkey dinner, or serve it alongside a roasted chicken (page 84) for a nice change of pace.

INGREDIENTS

2 recipes Savory Corn Bread (page 110), cooled

1 cup (225 g) unsalted butter or Earth Balance butter substitute, divided

2 packets (12 g each) turkey-flavored Savory Choice Liquid Broth Concentrate (optional, omit if not making the stuffing)

1 large onion, chopped

4 stalks celery, chopped

1 large shallot, sliced

10 large fresh sage leaves, finely chopped

Leaves from 2 sprigs fresh thyme

2 sweet apples, such as Gala or Fuji, washed, cored, and chopped

1½ cups (220 g) dried sweetened cranberries

1 cup (150 g) pecan halves, coarsely chopped

Kosher salt and freshly ground black pepper, to taste

1 egg, beaten

1½ to 2 cups (355 to 470 ml) turkey or chicken stock (page 136)

*There will be crumbs left over from making the stuffing.
Don't toss them out! Save them and use them as a
crumbly corn bread topping for your salad!*

METHOD

1. Preheat the oven to 400°F (200°C, or gas mark 6).

2. Cut the corn bread into ½-inch (1.3 cm) strips and then cut the strips crosswise into small cubes. Spread the cubes on a baking sheet.

3. Melt ¼ cup (56 g) of the butter and mix it with the turkey-flavored concentrate. Drizzle on top of the corn bread cubes. Toss gently and place in the oven. Bake the cubes for 30 minutes, stirring every 8 to 10 minutes, until they are toasted and completely dried out. (Note: This is very important for the texture of your final product. Make sure you toast the cubes thoroughly.) Remove from the oven and let cool to room temperature.

4. Turn the oven down to 350°F (180°C, or gas mark 4). Lightly butter a 9 x 13-inch (23 x 33 cm) baking pan; set aside.

5. In a large skillet, melt ¼ cup (56 g) of the butter over medium heat. Sauté the onion and celery for about 4 minutes and then add the shallot and sage. Continue cooking until the vegetables are softened and starting to brown, an additional 3 to 4 minutes. Remove from the heat and transfer to a large mixing bowl to cool.

6. Add the cooled corn bread cubes to the mixing bowl with the vegetables. Just use the cubes and leave behind the crumbs. (See the box on page 112.)

7. Add the thyme, apples, cranberries, and pecans to the corn bread mixture. Toss until evenly distributed. Melt the remaining ½ cup (112 g) butter in a microwave-safe bowl, then add it to the bowl and toss again. Taste and adjust the seasonings with salt and pepper. Stir in the beaten egg and turkey stock and transfer to the prepared baking pan.

8. Transfer to the oven and bake for about 45 minutes, or until the bread is golden brown and crusty on the top.

Yield: 6 to 8 servings

MASHED POTATOES

Gluten Free • Vegetarian • Soy Free • Nut Free

Mashed potatoes are the most versatile of side dishes. One of the best things about this recipe is you don't need to drain the potatoes after you cook them. Simply use an immersion blender to create smooth, fluffy mashed potatoes. To make garlic mashed potatoes, add several cloves of fresh, peeled, minced garlic to the potatoes and cook as directed! Serve with our Roast Turkey Breast and Easy Gravy (page 92), Southwestern Meatloaf (page 90), or your own favorite dishes. We love the flavor of red potatoes for mashed potatoes, but feel free to use any type of potato in this recipe.

INGREDIENTS

2 pounds (808 g) medium red potatoes, peeled and quartered

1 cup (235 ml) water

½ to ¾ cup (120 to 180 ml) milk

¼ cup (56 g) unsalted butter

¼ teaspoon salt

¼ teaspoon cracked black pepper

You can easily double this recipe without adding extra cook time. Even though the time doesn't double, you'll need to double the seasonings so the flavor doesn't get diluted.

METHOD

1. Add the potatoes and water to the inner pot of your electric pressure cooker.

2. Close and lock the lid, making sure the steam release knob is in the sealing position. Cook on high pressure for 10 minutes. When the cook time is finished, do a quick pressure release by safely moving the sealing knob to the venting position and allowing the steam to escape. When the float pin drops, unlock the lid and open it carefully.

3. Add the milk, butter, salt, and pepper to the potatoes. No need to take out the potatoes to drain them; you can mash them in the pot. Use an immersion blender or potato masher and mash until the desired consistency is reached. Taste and adjust the seasonings as needed.

4. Serve with your favorite gluten-free gravy or an extra pat of butter!

Yield: 4 servings

DELIGHTFUL DESSERTS

Eating gluten free doesn't mean you can't indulge your sweet tooth with delightful and decadent desserts. We make no apologies about loving dessert. Anything and everything chocolate for us, please! While using an electric pressure cooker for "baking" isn't immediately obvious, it is one of the best features.

When you cover a baking dish, the heat in the pressure cooker creates an oven-like setting. Using steam creates a moister environment, which is especially well suited for cheesecakes. If you've ever fought with a leaking springform pan in a pan of water, you will love the results you get in today's pressure cookers!

The key to successful gluten-free baking is a gluten-free flour blend. We've included a recipe to make your own blend (less expensive if you bake often), or you can use a store-bought variety. A few of our favorites are Bob's Red Mill 1-to-1, Cup4Cup, and Pamela's All-Purpose Gluten-Free Flour, all readily available in grocery stores and online.

Enjoy our Double Chocolate Fudge Cheesecake (page 128), Mexican Chocolate Pound Cake (page 130), Apple Cinnamon Raisin Bread Pudding (page 118), and more, all made gluten free. For the times you don't want to share, you can make Individual Key Lime Cheesecakes (page 124). Just be sure to hide the evidence or they will disappear before you know it!

Our collection of dessert recipes will have you and your family racing back to the table for seconds. You may have to live gluten free, but that doesn't mean having to sacrifice flavor or special desserts.

APPLE CINNAMON RAISIN BREAD PUDDING

Gluten Free • Soy Free • Vegetarian

Bread pudding is an all-time favorite dessert. This homemade version is packed with fruit and has a sweet, fluffy custard and a sinfully delicious vanilla sauce that is caramel-like in consistency. We call it perfection on a plate and because it's made with gluten-free cinnamon raisin bread, we can enjoy it anytime!

INGREDIENTS

For the bread pudding

2 tablespoons (28 g) unsalted butter, melted, plus more for the pan

½ cup (100 g) dark brown sugar

2½ cups (590 ml) whole milk

4 eggs, beaten

2 teaspoons (10 ml) gluten-free vanilla extract

1 teaspoon ground cinnamon

½ teaspoon ground nutmeg

¼ teaspoon salt

8 cups (400 g) cubed gluten-free cinnamon raisin bread (such as Udi's brand)

½ cup (75 g) chopped pecans, toasted

2 medium baking apples (Honeycrisp or Braeburn work beautifully), peeled, cored, and chopped into a medium dice

1½ cups (355 ml) water

For the sweet vanilla sauce

½ cup (112 g) unsalted butter

½ cup (100 g) granulated sugar

½ cup (100 g) dark brown sugar

¼ teaspoon salt

1 tablespoon (15 ml) gluten-free vanilla extract

½ cup (120 ml) heavy whipping cream

If you can't find gluten-free cinnamon raisin bread, you can substitute any other hearty gluten-free bread and add ½ cup (75 g) raisins and an extra 3 tablespoons (36 g) sugar to the recipe.

METHOD

Bread Pudding

1. In a large bowl, whisk together the 2 tablespoons (28 g) butter, brown sugar, milk, eggs, vanilla, spices, and salt. Add the cubed bread, toasted nuts, and apple pieces. Mix until well combined. Set aside while you prepare the pan.

2. Using either a 6-cup (1410 ml) Bundt or 1½-quart (1.4 L) round baking dish, butter the bottom and sides of the pan. Be sure to get into the corners of the pan. Pour the bread pudding mixture into the prepared pan.

3. Place a trivet in your pressure cooker. Add the water to the bottom of the pot. Spray a piece of aluminum foil with nonstick cooking spray and place (sprayed side down) over the bread pudding. This will protect the pudding from excess moisture while cooking. Use a foil sling (see page 15) to lower the bread pudding onto the trivet.

4. Close and lock the lid, making sure the steam release knob is in the sealing position. Cook on high pressure for 25 minutes. When the cook time is finished, use the quick release method by turning the release knob to the venting position and releasing the steam. Once the float pin drops, unlock the lid and open it carefully.

5. Use the foil sling to remove the dish from the pressure cooker. If you like a crispy top, place your dish on a sheet pan and put in the oven at 400°F (200°C, or gas mark 6) for 5 minutes. Watch the bread pudding carefully so it doesn't get too brown.

Sweet Vanilla Sauce

1. While the bread pudding is in the oven, or during the last 10 minutes of cooking time, make the sweet vanilla sauce. In a small pan, combine all the sauce ingredients. Place over medium heat, stirring constantly, until the butter has fully melted and the sauce thickens, 5 to 8 minutes.

2. Cut the bread pudding into pieces, then pour some sauce over each piece. Serve warm and try not to lick the spoon!

Yield: 6 servings

NEW YORK–STYLE CHEESECAKE

Gluten Free • Soy Free

This is a lovely adaptation of a classic New York–style cheesecake. Using ground almond meal and brown sugar in place of graham crackers will remind you of the flavors of a traditional graham cracker crust without the gluten. The pressure cooker mimics the process of baking cheesecake in a water bath, and the moisture inside the pressure cooker helps reduce the possibility of your cheesecake developing cracks. For the smoothest possible cheesecake, make sure all your ingredients are at room temperature before you begin.

INGREDIENTS

For the crust

2 cups (224 g) almond meal (Bob's Red Mill brand is certified gluten free)

¼ teaspoon salt

1½ tablespoons (18 g) brown sugar

¼ cup (56 g) unsalted butter, melted

For the cheesecake

1 pound (454 g) cream cheese, at room temperature

2 tablespoons (16 g) cornstarch

⅔ cup (128 g) granulated sugar

Pinch of salt

½ cup (120 g) sour cream, at room temperature

2 teaspoons (10 ml) gluten-free vanilla extract

⅛ teaspoon gluten-free almond extract

2 large eggs, at room temperature

1 cup (235 ml) cold water

Use a 7 x 3-inch (18 x 7.6 cm) springform or push pan for this recipe. It fits perfectly in the inner pot of a 6-quart (5.4 L) pressure cooker and can be used for a variety of sweet or savory recipes!

METHOD

Crust

1. Lightly spray the bottom and sides of a 7 x 3-inch (18 x 7.6 cm) springform pan with nonstick cooking spray (the kind without flour in it).

2. Cut a circle of parchment paper the same size as the bottom of your springform pan. Place the parchment circle on the bottom of your pan and lightly spray with additional nonstick spray. Set aside.

3. In a small bowl, mix together the almond meal, salt, and brown sugar. Add the melted butter and stir with a fork until it sticks together.

4. Pour the crust mixture into the prepared pan. Spread with your fingers and press down gently to form an even layer. Place the pan in the freezer while you make the cheesecake batter.

Cheesecake

1. In a medium mixing bowl, beat the cream cheese with a hand mixer on low speed, until smooth. In a small mixing bowl, combine the cornstarch, granulated sugar, and salt. Add half the sugar mixture to the cream cheese and beat until just incorporated. Scrape down the sides of your bowl with a spatula. Add the remaining sugar mixture and beat until just incorporated. Add the sour cream and vanilla and almond extracts to the cream cheese mixture. Beat until it just comes together.

2. Add the eggs, one at a time, scraping down the bowl well after each addition. Do not overmix.

3. Remove the crust from the freezer. Tightly wrap the bottom of the pan with aluminum foil to help prevent leaks. Pour the cream cheese batter over the crust. Tap lightly on the countertop to remove air bubbles.

4. Pour the cold water into the inner pot of your pressure cooker. Place a trivet in the pot. Use a foil sling (see page 15) to carefully place the cheesecake pan on top of the trivet. Make sure the pan is not touching the water.

5. Close and lock the lid, making sure the steam release knob is in the sealing position. Cook on high pressure for 40 minutes. When finished, use the quick release method by turning the release knob to the venting position and releasing the steam. Once the float pin drops, unlock the lid and open it carefully. Gently blot the surface of the cheesecake with a paper towel to absorb any condensation.

6. Carefully remove the cheesecake and place it on a wire rack to cool.

7. Once the cheesecake is completely cooled, place in the refrigerator for 6 to 8 hours or overnight. When ready to serve, remove the cheesecake from the refrigerator. Release the sides of the springform pan and run a thin knife between the parchment paper and the crust, and then slide carefully onto a serving plate.

Yield: One 7-inch (18 cm) cheesecake

RICE PUDDING WITH RAISINS

Gluten Free • Nut Free • Soy Free • Vegetarian

This rice pudding is sweet, thick, and so creamy you may have to use a fork to eat it. This recipe uses raisins, but feel free to make it your own by adding different dried fruits or nuts. It would be great with dried mango or cranberries. The raisins don't have to be soaked in boiling water—you can soak them in orange juice or even apple juice for a sweeter flavor. If you can't find Arborio rice, use any short-grain (not instant) white rice.

INGREDIENTS

1 cup (150 g) raisins

1 cup (235 ml) boiling water

1½ cups (270 g) Arborio rice

¾ cup (144 g) sugar

½ teaspoon salt

5 cups (1175 ml) milk

2 eggs

1 cup (235 ml) half-and-half

2 teaspoons (10 ml) gluten-free vanilla extract

METHOD

1. In a medium bowl, combine the raisins and boiling water. Cover and set aside for 30 minutes to plump the raisins. Note: If using juice or other liquid to plump the raisins, you do not need to boil the liquid. Just cover and soak for at least 30 minutes or up to 2 days in the refrigerator.

2. Combine the rice, sugar, salt, and milk in the inner pot of your electric pressure cooker. Press Sauté or Browning and bring to a boil, stirring constantly to dissolve the sugar. As soon as the mixture comes to a boil, press Cancel, then close and lock the lid, making sure the steam release knob is in the sealing position.

3. Cook on low pressure for 15 minutes. When the rice is finished, allow a 10-minute natural pressure release. After 10 minutes, turn the knob to the venting position, releasing any remaining steam. When the float pin drops, unlock the lid and open it carefully. Press Cancel.

4. While the rice is cooling, whisk together the eggs, half-and-half, and vanilla in a medium bowl. Carefully pour the mixture into the pot with the rice. Stir to combine. Turn the pressure cooker back on, selecting Sauté or Browning. Stir until the rice just begins to boil.

5. When the rice is hot, drain the raisins from their soaking liquid and stir into the pot. Serve immediately or pour into a large serving dish to chill. The pudding will thicken as it cools, so you may want to add a little extra half-and-half if you plan on serving it cold.

Yield: 6 servings

INDIVIDUAL KEY LIME CHEESECAKES

Gluten Free • Nut Free • Soy Free

It's a lot of fun to create individual desserts in your pressure cooker. Make them to share at a party or to keep dessert to yourself for an entire week. Key limes are smaller than regular limes and have a stronger, more acidic flavor. They make the perfect summer cheesecake, as the harvest season in the United States for Key limes is relatively short. For the smoothest possible cheesecake batter, ensure all your ingredients are at room temperature before you begin.

INGREDIENTS

For the crust

1¼ cups (125 g) ground gluten-free shortbread cookies (such as Pamela's brand)

1½ teaspoons brown sugar

2 tablespoons (28 g) unsalted butter, melted

Pinch of salt

For the cheesecake

8 ounces (227 g) cream cheese, at room temperature

1 tablespoon (8 g) cornstarch

⅓ cup (65 g) granulated sugar

Pinch of salt

1 tablespoon (15 ml) Key lime juice

¼ cup (60 g) sour cream, at room temperature

1 teaspoon gluten-free vanilla extract

1 tablespoon (6 g) finely grated Key lime zest, plus more for garnishing

1 large egg, at room temperature

1½ cups (355 ml) water

Whipped cream, for garnishing

This recipe calls for 4-ounce (115 g) canning jars, sometimes called quilted jelly jars. If you don't have canning jars, you can use 4-ounce (115 g) glass ramekins.

METHOD

Crust

1. Lightly spray the insides of six 4-ounce (115 g) mason jars with nonstick cooking spray.

2. In a small bowl, mix together the crushed cookies, brown sugar, butter, and salt. Divide the cookie mixture evenly among the mason jars. Gently press the cookie crust against the bottom of the glasses.

Cheesecake

1. In a medium mixing bowl, beat the cream cheese with a hand mixer on low speed, until smooth. In a small mixing bowl, combine the cornstarch, granulated sugar, and salt. Add the sugar mixture to the cream cheese and beat until just incorporated. Scrape down the sides of the bowl with a spatula.

2. Add the lime juice, sour cream, vanilla, and lime zest to the cream cheese mixture. Beat until it just comes together. Add the egg; stir until just combined. Do not overmix.

3. Divide the cheesecake batter equally among the jars. Lightly tap the jars against the counter to release any large air bubbles.

4. Add the water to the bottom of the inner pot. Place a trivet inside the pot. Place the filled jars on the trivet, being careful the sides of the jars don't touch each other or the sides of the pot. You should be able to fit five around the edges and have space for one jar in the middle. Lightly place a large piece of foil over all the jars.

5. Close and lock the lid, making sure the steam release knob is in the sealing position. Cook on high pressure for 4 minutes. When the cook time is finished, allow a natural release for 10 minutes, then move the knob to the venting position and release any remaining steam. When the float pin drops, unlock the lid and open it carefully. Press Cancel.

6. Remove the foil and absorb any condensation on the surface of the cheesecakes by gently blotting with a paper towel. Allow the cheesecakes to cool inside the pot for 30 minutes, then remove to a cooling rack and let cool until they reach room temperature. Cover the cheesecakes with plastic wrap and place in the refrigerator for at least 6 to 8 hours, preferably overnight.

7. Serve garnished with whipped cream and additional lime zest.

Yield: 6 individual cheesecakes

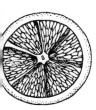

SWEET SPICED APPLESAUCE

Gluten Free • Dairy Free • Soy Free • Nut Free • Vegetarian • Vegan

A variety of apples will give your applesauce the best possible flavor. Our favorites are Honeycrisp, Fuji, and Braeburn, as they hold up well in the pressure cooker. No need to peel your apples for this recipe. The peels add extra nutrients, color, and flavor. The peels will get soft in the pressure cooker and then practically dissolve when blended into the applesauce. Apples tend to give off a lot of water, so you'll only need to add ¼ cup (60 ml) of liquid to make this recipe work. Once you see how simple this sweet applesauce is to make, you may never buy it from the store again.

INGREDIENTS

3 pounds (1.4 kg) assorted apples, cored and quartered

¼ cup (60 ml) water or unsweetened apple juice

2 whole cinnamon sticks

1 tablespoon (20 g) honey or 2 tablespoons (24 g) brown sugar (optional)

1½ tablespoons (10 g) ground cinnamon

¼ teaspoon ground nutmeg

We suggest avoiding Red Delicious apples; while they are fine to eat, they don't retain a lot of flavor when they are cooked and the texture tends to get grainy.

METHOD

1. Place all the ingredients in the inner pot of your electric pressure cooker.

2. Close and lock the lid, making sure the steam release knob is in the sealing position. Cook on high pressure for 5 minutes. Once the cook time is finished, allow for a complete natural release. This should take about 15 minutes. When the float pin has dropped, unlock the lid and open it carefully.

3. Remove the cinnamon sticks. Using an immersion blender, puree the apples to your desired consistency. If you don't have an immersion blender, you can use a food processor or countertop blender. Just be sure to blend in batches, as the applesauce will be quite hot!

4. Let cool and serve!

Yield: 8 cups (1960 g)

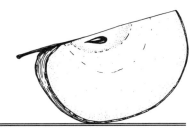

DOUBLE CHOCOLATE FUDGE CHEESECAKE

Gluten Free • Nut Free • Soy Free

Two different layers of chocolate make this cheesecake every chocolate lover's dream come true. Dense and rich, a small slice goes a long way! Make sure your cream cheese is at room temperature to be completely smooth. If the cream cheese is not at room temperature, you could wind up with small white flecks in your chocolate cheesecake. When ready to serve, use a very sharp knife, dipped in hot water after each cut, to create beautifully clean slices.

INGREDIENTS

For the crust

1 (6.1-ounce, or 171 g) box gluten-free chocolate cookies

1 tablespoon (12 g) granulated sugar

¼ teaspoon salt

2 tablespoons (28 g) unsalted butter, melted

For the cheesecake

1¼ cups (219 g) semisweet chocolate chips

1 pound (454 g) cream cheese, at room temperature

¾ cup (144 g) granulated sugar

3 large eggs, at room temperature

¼ cup (60 g) sour cream

2 teaspoons (10 ml) gluten-free vanilla extract

1½ cups (355 ml) water

Confectioner's sugar, for dusting

We used Enjoy Life Double Chocolate Handcrafted Crunchy Cookies. Feel free to substitute your favorite gluten-free chocolate cookies.

METHOD

Crust

1. Spray a 7 x 3-inch (18 x 7.6 cm) springform pan with nonstick cooking spray. Cut a parchment circle the same size as the bottom of the pan and place it inside your pan. Spray the parchment. Set aside.

2. Place the cookies in the bowl of a food processor and pulse until they resemble coarse sand. Pour the cookie crumbs into a medium bowl and add the sugar and salt. Stir to combine. Add the melted butter and stir until the mixture sticks together.

3. Gently press the crumbs evenly on the bottom of the prepared pan. Use your fingers or a flat-bottom glass to help press the crust in place. Put the crust in the freezer while you make the filling.

Cheesecake

1. In a medium microwave-safe bowl, melt the chocolate chips on high power, stirring every 30 seconds, until smooth and completely melted. Let cool slightly.

2. In the bowl of a stand mixer, beat the cream cheese until smooth. Add the ¾ cup (144 g) granulated sugar and continue to beat. Add the eggs, one at a time, beating for 1 minute and scraping down the sides of the bowl after each addition. Beat in the sour cream and vanilla until fully incorporated.

3. With the mixer on low speed, slowly add the cooled melted chocolate. Mix in completely. Pour the filling into the prepared crust. Tap the dish on the counter to remove air bubbles.

4. Place a trivet in the bottom of the inner pot of your pressure cooker and add the water.

5. Tightly wrap the bottom of the springform pan in aluminum foil. Lightly spray a piece of foil with nonstick cooking spray and place (sprayed side down) over the cheesecake. Using a foil sling (see page 15), lower the pot onto the trivet.

6. Close and lock the lid, making sure the steam release knob is in the sealing position. Cook on high pressure for 56 minutes. When it is finished, use a quick release by turning the release knob to the venting position, releasing all the steam. When the float pin drops, unlock the lid and open it carefully. Press Cancel.

7. Using the foil sling, carefully move the cheesecake to a wire cooling rack. After 1 hour, remove the foil and run a thin knife around the edges of the cheesecake to loosen it from the pan.

8. Cover with plastic wrap and refrigerate for at least 8 hours or overnight, until fully set.

9. Cut into 8 slices and serve with a sprinkle of confectioner's sugar on top.

Yield: 8 slices

MEXICAN CHOCOLATE POUND CAKE

Gluten Free • Soy Free • Nut Free

There are simply times when your craving for chocolate needs to be satisfied. This rich, moist, dense cake with a glossy chocolate glaze is perfect for satisfying those hankerings. We've replicated the flavor profile of Mexican chocolate by using semisweet chocolate and plenty of cinnamon. Try pairing this pound cake with a cup of coffee on a rainy afternoon. Make it extra fancy by adding whipped cream to the top!

INGREDIENTS

1½ cups (355 ml) water

1 cup (175 g) semisweet chocolate chips, divided

¼ cup (56 g) unsalted butter, softened

1 cup (192 g) sugar

2 large eggs, at room temperature

⅓ cup (80 ml) chocolate syrup

1 tablespoon (15 ml) gluten-free vanilla extract

1⅓ cups (160 g) All-Purpose Gluten-Free Flour Blend (page 19)

½ teaspoon baking soda

1 tablespoon (7 g) ground cinnamon

¼ teaspoon salt

½ cup (120 ml) buttermilk, divided

2 tablespoons (30 ml) heavy cream

METHOD

1. Pour the water into the inner pot of your pressure cooker. Add a trivet to the pot. Spray a 7 x 3-inch (18 x 7.6 cm) springform pan with nonstick cooking spray. Set aside.

2. Place ⅔ cup (115 g) of the chocolate chips in a microwave-safe bowl. Microwave on high power at 30-second intervals until the chocolate is melted and smooth, stirring well each time. Set aside.

3. In the bowl of a stand mixer, beat the butter and sugar for 6 minutes, or until the mixture is light and fluffy. Add the eggs, one at a time, beating well after each addition. Add the chocolate syrup, vanilla, and melted chocolate chips and beat until well blended.

4. In a medium bowl, whisk together the flour blend, baking soda, cinnamon, and salt. With your mixer at low speed, add half the flour mixture to the chocolate batter, blending well. Add ¼ cup (60 ml) of the buttermilk, and blend. Add the remaining flour mixture and then the rest of the buttermilk, continuing to beat at low speed until the mixture is just combined.

5. Pour the batter into the prepared pan. Spray one side of a piece of aluminum foil with nonstick cooking spray and cover the cake (sprayed side down), crimping the edges to seal. Using a foil sling (see page 15), lower the cake onto the trivet in your pressure cooker.

6. Close and lock the lid, making sure the steam release knob is in the sealing position. Cook on high pressure for 55 minutes. When the cook time is finished, allow a 10-minute natural release, then turn the knob to the venting position, releasing any remaining steam. When the float pin drops, unlock the lid and open it carefully.

7. Using the foil sling, lift the cake from the pot and place on a wire cooling rack. Remove the foil from the top and allow the cake to cool for 10 minutes. Using a narrow spatula or a slim knife, gently loosen the cake from the sides of the pan and invert onto the cooling rack. Allow to cool completely.

8. After the cake is cool, make the glaze. Microwave the remaining ⅓ cup (60 g) chocolate chips in a microwave-safe bowl at high power for 2 minutes, stirring after every 30 seconds, until smooth. Add the heavy cream and microwave for an additional 15 seconds, or until just warm through. Stir until smooth and glossy. Drizzle the glaze over the cake. Allow the cake to stand for an additional 30 minutes to 1 hour for the glaze to set before serving.

Yield: 8 servings

BASIC STOCKS

The foundation of many recipes is a full-bodied stock. Whether chicken, beef, or vegetable, stocks provide a tremendous boost to your recipes. You can use them for soups, stews, and sauces or to add flavor and protein to grains. They are also a great way to use leftover bones from steaks and roasts, the carcass from your chicken or turkey dinner, and the trimmings from your vegetables.

Rather than using water as a base, try a stock as the liquid in your cooking. You may be surprised at the depth of flavor you get, transforming your dish into something that might be served in a restaurant.

Today's electric pressure cookers give you the same taste as if you had simmered the stock for hours on the stove, but in a fraction of the time. Preheating the liquid will cut down on the time it takes to bring the pot to pressure because it is closer to the boiling point. Use the Sauté feature to warm your liquids while you are prepping and adding the remaining ingredients.

If your children don't like eating vegetables, using a vegetable stock will give them a natural dose of vitamins and minerals without them knowing! Whenever you are cooking, save the extra vegetable parings and tuck them in a resealable bag in the freezer. Keep adding to the bag and, when you have enough, you can make a quick stock. Likewise, if you have extra meat or bones left over from a chicken dinner, you can do the same thing. If you don't have a use for the stock right away, or have extra, freeze it for a last-minute addition that will elevate your cooking.

BEEF STOCK

Gluten Free • Dairy Free • Nut Free • Egg Free

The difference between canned and homemade stock is dramatic. Homemade is so much richer and more meaty. This beef stock can be used to make Beef "Barley" Soup with Sorghum (page 44) and a number of other recipes. Make this ahead and freeze in smaller amounts to have it readily available whenever you feel like cooking.

INGREDIENTS

2 pounds (908 g) beef bones, cut into smaller pieces

1 pound (454 g) beef chuck, cut into large cubes

1 large yellow onion, quartered

3 carrots, trimmed and coarsely chopped

2 stalks celery, trimmed and coarsely chopped

1 sprig fresh rosemary, well rinsed

2 bay leaves

2 tablespoons (10 g) gluten-free beef base (such as Herb-Ox brand), dissolved in ½ cup (120 ml) hot water

1 teaspoon whole black peppercorns

4½ cups (1058 ml) warm water

When you are making soups and stocks, the pressure cooker will take longer to come to pressure because you have to bring all the liquid to a boil to create the steam it needs. Be patient; the wait will be worth it when you taste the depth of flavor in your recipes!

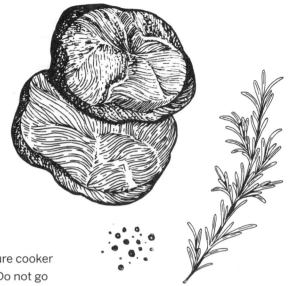

METHOD

1. Place the bones in the inner pot of your electric pressure cooker and add the remaining ingredients in the order given. Do not go over the maximum fill line on your pot!

2. Close and lock the lid, making sure the steam release handle is in the sealing position. Cook on high pressure for 2 hours. Once the machine has come to pressure, the clock will count down.

3. When it is finished, let the pressure release naturally. Turn the steam release handle to the venting position, releasing any remaining steam. Unlock the lid and open it carefully.

4. Set a colander over a very large bowl and strain the stock. Discard the solids. Refrigerate the stock. When the fat hardens, skim off and discard. Refrigerate for up to 3 days or freeze for longer storage.

Yield: About 5 cups (1175 ml)

CHICKEN STOCK

Gluten Free • Dairy Free • Soy Free • Nut Free • Egg Free

A pot of homemade stock made from bones and "spare parts" is rich in flavor and nutrients. You can use it to make soup, to add flavor and protein to cooked grains, or as the base for a rich stew. Keep smaller portions in the freezer for quick weeknight meals.

INGREDIENTS

1 chicken carcass plus wings, backs, necks, etc. (about 2 pounds, or 908 g, total weight)

5 cups (1175 ml) cool water

1 large yellow onion, quartered

3 carrots, trimmed and coarsely chopped

2 stalks celery, trimmed and coarsely chopped

4 sprigs fresh thyme

2 teaspoons (12 g) kosher or fine sea salt

1 teaspoon whole black peppercorns

This same technique can be used to make turkey stock after Thanksgiving or any time of the year. Just add sage leaves to get that classic flavor. Divide the stock into smaller portions, place in resealable bags, and freeze flat on a baking sheet. When solid, you can stack the bags in your freezer and pull out just what you need for any recipe.

METHOD

1. Place the chicken carcass and parts in the inner pot of your pressure cooker. Add the water and the remaining ingredients.

2. Close and lock the lid, making sure the steam release handle is in the sealing position. Cook on high pressure for 60 minutes. When the cook time is finished, let the pressure naturally release for 12 minutes, then turn the steam release handle to the venting position, releasing any remaining steam. Unlock the lid and open it carefully.

3. Set a colander over a very large bowl or cooking pot and carefully pour the stock through. Discard the solids. Refrigerate, covered, for up to 3 days or freeze for longer storage.

Yield: About 5 cups (1175 ml)

VEGETABLE STOCK

Gluten Free • Dairy Free • Vegetarian • Vegan • Soy Free • Nut Free • Egg Free

For a bolder vegetable flavor, use this stock as the base for recipes such as soups, vegetable stews, and vegetarian meals. It's so satisfying that your guests will not care there isn't meat in the dish!

INGREDIENTS

1 large onion, coarsely chopped

4 carrots, trimmed and cut into chunks

5 stalks celery, coarsely chopped

2 cups (140 g) sliced mushrooms

1 tablespoon (15 g) tomato paste dissolved in ¼ cup (60 ml) water

1 clove garlic, sliced

2 bay leaves

2 sprigs fresh thyme

3 sprigs fresh parsley

1 teaspoon kosher or fine sea salt

1 teaspoon whole peppercorns

About 6 cups (1410 ml) water

While you can use small bits of leftover vegetables to make a broth, avoid cruciferous vegetables (cabbage, cauliflower, broccoli, Brussels sprouts, bok choy, etc.) because they add bitterness to your broth, making it unusable.

METHOD

1. Place all the vegetables and seasonings in the inner pot of your electric pressure cooker. Add enough water to cover the ingredients by about 1 inch (2.5 cm). Close and lock the lid, making sure the steam release handle is in the sealing position. Cook at high pressure for 18 minutes. When the cook time is finished, let the pressure naturally release for 15 minutes, then turn the steam release handle to the venting position, releasing any remaining steam. Unlock the lid and open it carefully.

2. Set a colander over a very large bowl or cooking pot and strain the stock, pressing on the solids to extract all the liquid. Discard the solids. Taste and adjust the seasonings if needed. Refrigerate for up to 3 days or freeze for longer storage.

Yield: About 6 cups (1410 ml)

Acknowledgments

From Jane

Thanks to the great team at Harvard Common Press/The Quarto Group, including Dan Rosenberg, Meredith Quinn, Karen Levy, Kristine Anderson, and Anne Re for their support, partnership, and help in making this book a reality. Thank you for your belief in us and helping make this process smooth and easy. To Leslie Stoker, agent extraordinaire: Thank you for helping guide us through this project, being our advocate and ardent supporter. We are delighted to be a part of your talented group of authors. And to Sara, my friend and fabulous partner in this crazy ride we call writing a cookbook: Your expertise and skill with pressure cooking, your positive attitude, and your joyful spirit are remarkable. An extraordinary teammate, it was a pleasure working together to create and shape this book.

From Sara

To Kim Peeples, at VomFASS Claremont, for saying "Let's have an Instant Pot Class!" and starting me down this path. Your friendship and leadership example mean so much! To Kimberly Grant, recipe tester extraordinaire, who tested while selling her house, buying a new one, and moving her family across the entire country. I am so grateful! To our agent Leslie Stoker, who handled things (including us) quickly, effortlessly, and gracefully. To Dan Rosenberg, Meredith Quinn, Karen Levy, and the entire publishing team at Harvard Common Press: Thank you for seeing the vision of this book and working so hard to make it happen. To Robert Schueller and Melissa's Produce for your unwavering support. And of course, to Jane, my friend and coauthor. Thank you for sharing this project with me and having the confidence to put my name beside yours on the cover.

About the Authors

Jane Bonacci is the founder and author of *The Heritage Cook* food blog and coauthor of *The Gluten-Free Bread Machine Cookbook*. She is an expert in gluten-free baking and cooking, as well as a professional food writer and recipe developer, editor, and tester. She lives with her husband in the San Francisco Bay Area.

Sara De Leeuw is a culinary instructor, freelance writer, and professional recipe tester/developer who has captured the appetites of readers on her food blog *My Imperfect Kitchen!* She teaches private cooking classes, hosts live public cooking demos, and has been a judge for multiple food competitions. A member of the International Association of Culinary Professionals, she is happiest in the kitchen, sharing recipes and trying new and different cuisines. When she's not teaching or writing, you can find her doting over her two adorable grandchildren.

INDEX